BAMUSERS
MUSINGS IN ART

BRUCE ARLEN

ArlenArts
Cave Creek

BAMUSERS: MUSINGS IN ART

Author: Bruce Arlen
Cover and Book Design: Marty Safir

Published by
ArlenArts
P.O. Box 4023
Cave Creek, Arizona 85327

www.bamusers.com

ISBN 978-0-9913007-0-9

9 8 7 6 5 4 3 2 1

For Lisa, my biggest cheerleader, best
advisor, and love of my life!
And for Sari who I miss every day.

*E*njoy these expressions of human nature. A cavalcade of people, animals, objects, and more live on these pages. May the *Bamusers*, as I call them, bring you some thoughtful double takes, but most importantly, spontaneous amusement.

Happy viewing,

Bruce Arlen

Bruce Arlen

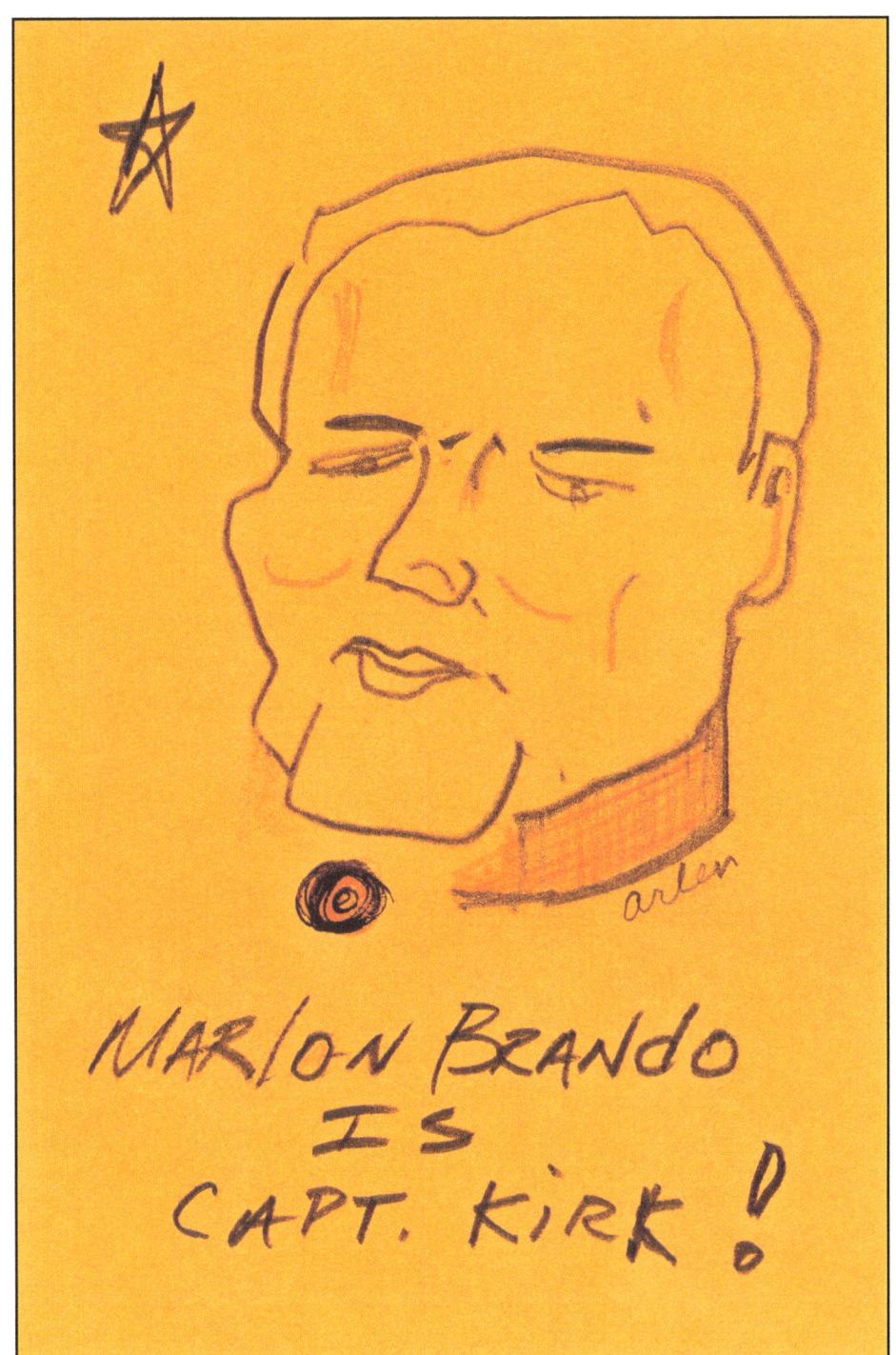

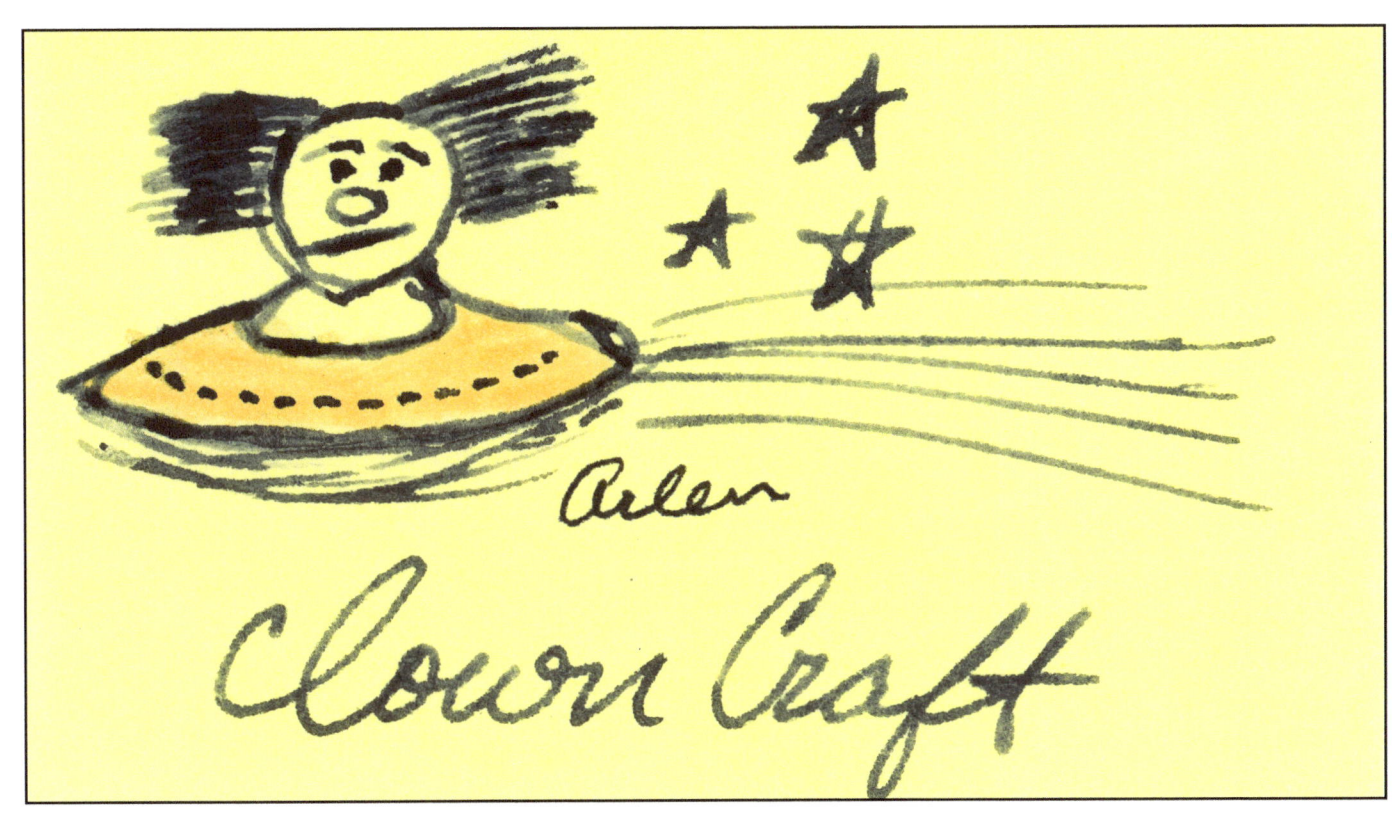

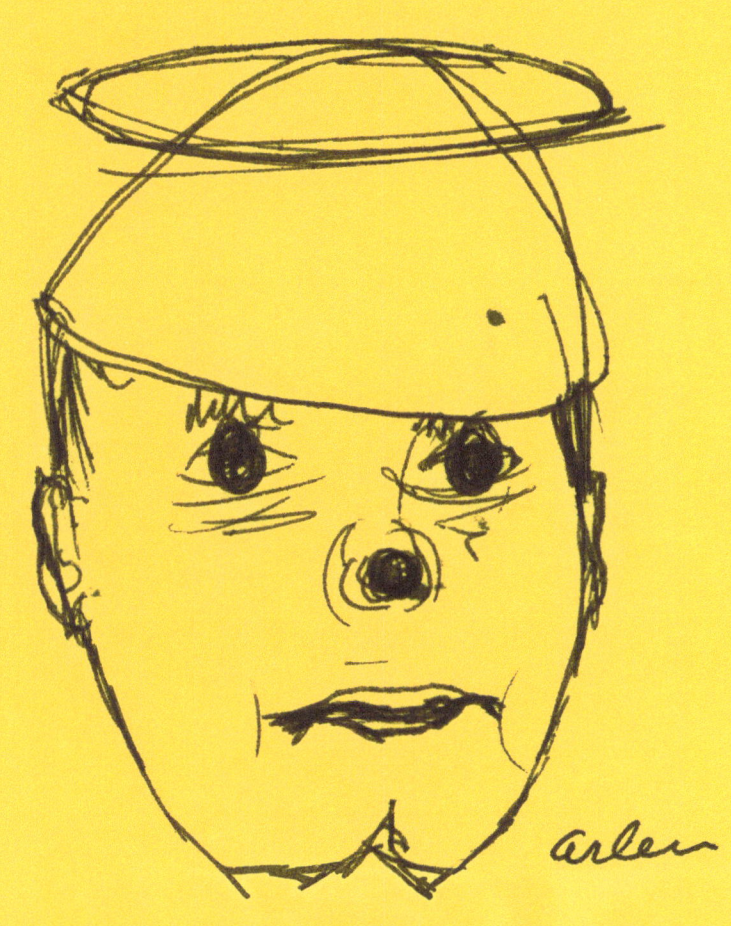

My Science Teacher Made me
Who I am today!

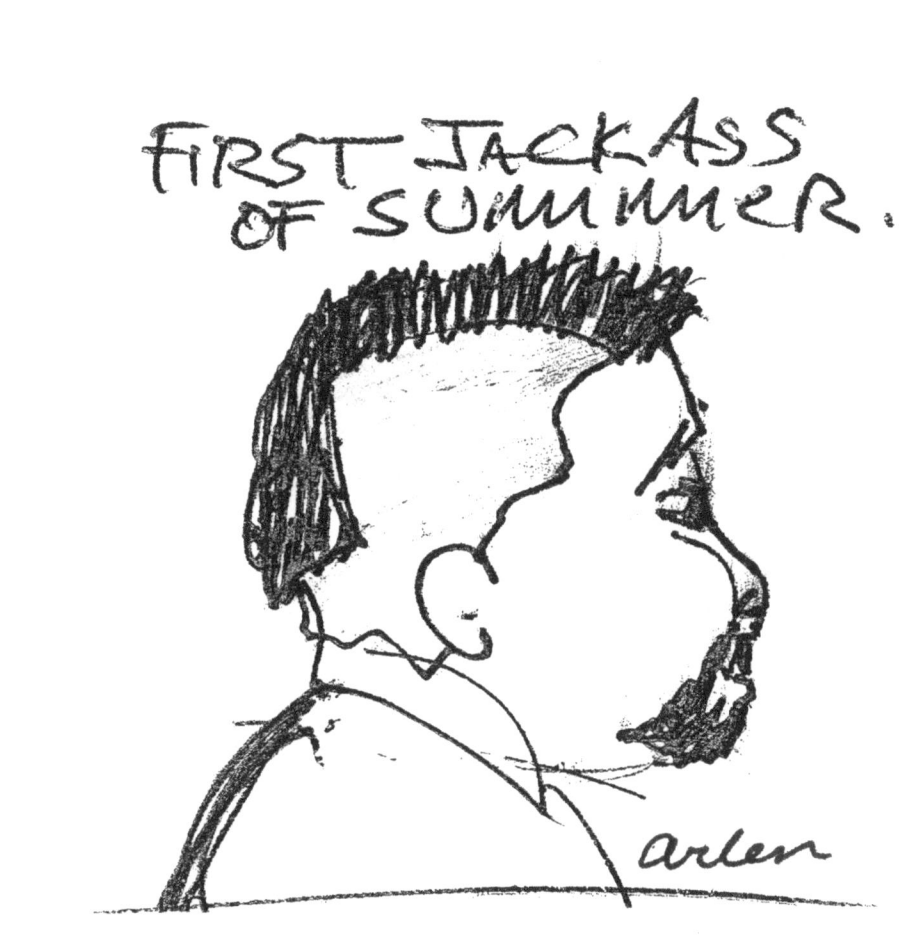

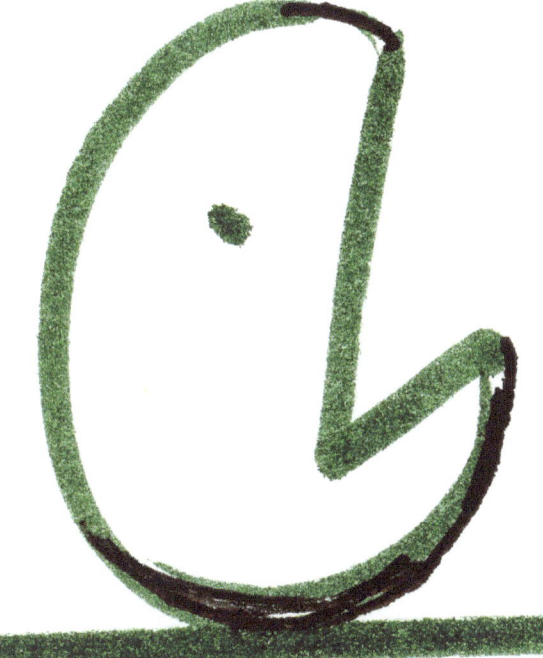

arlen

"THE Screaming
PacMAN"

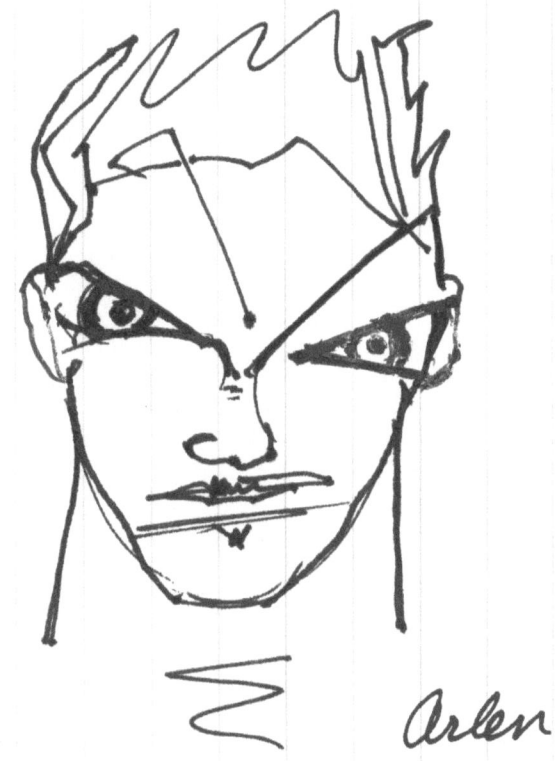

Arlen

Super Hero Academy
HRS: MON-FRI   10AM-4PM

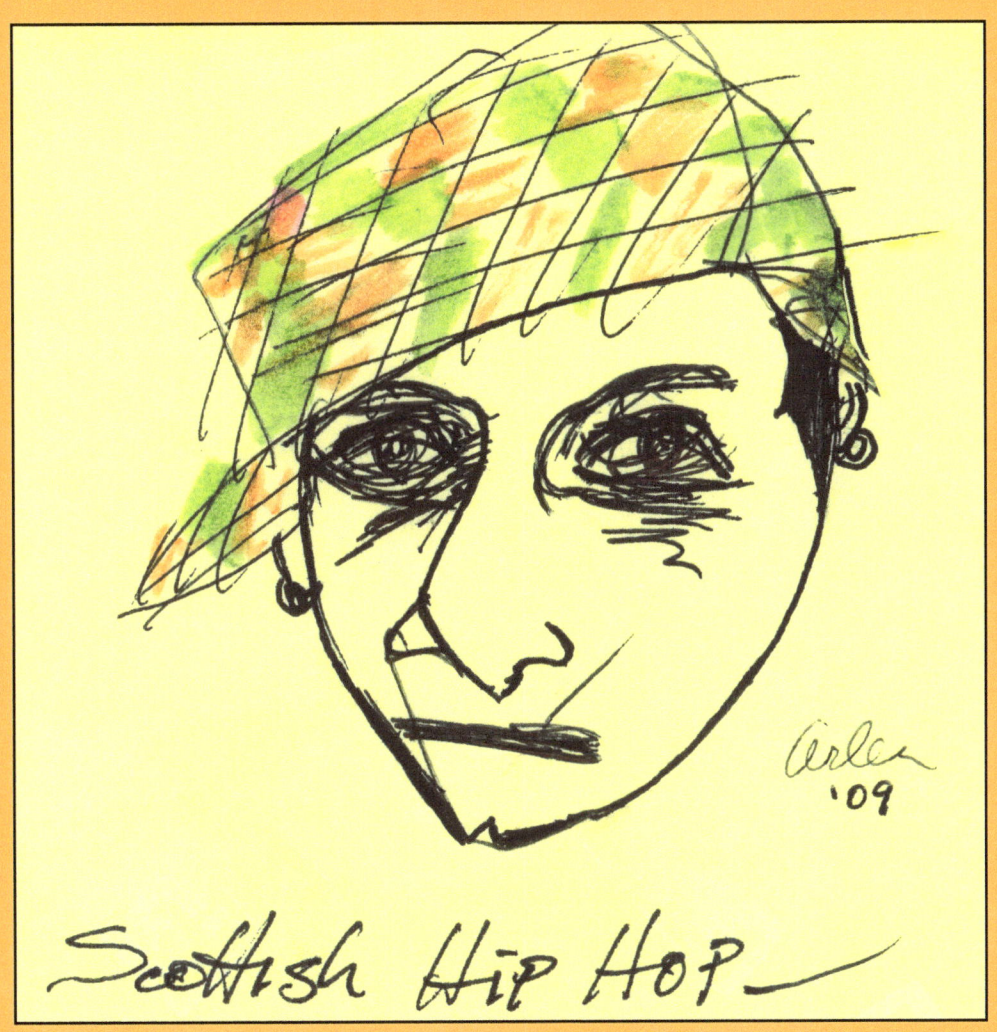

Scottish Hip Hop

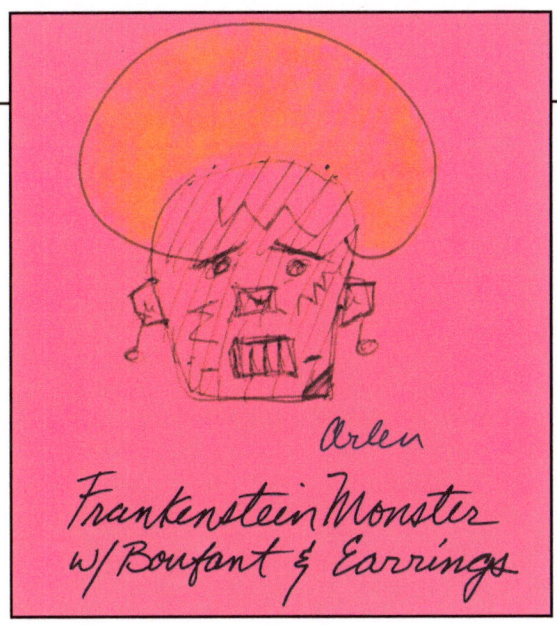

arlen

Frankenstein Monster
w/ Boufant & Earrings

Frankenstein Monster
in POLO Shirt & Slacks

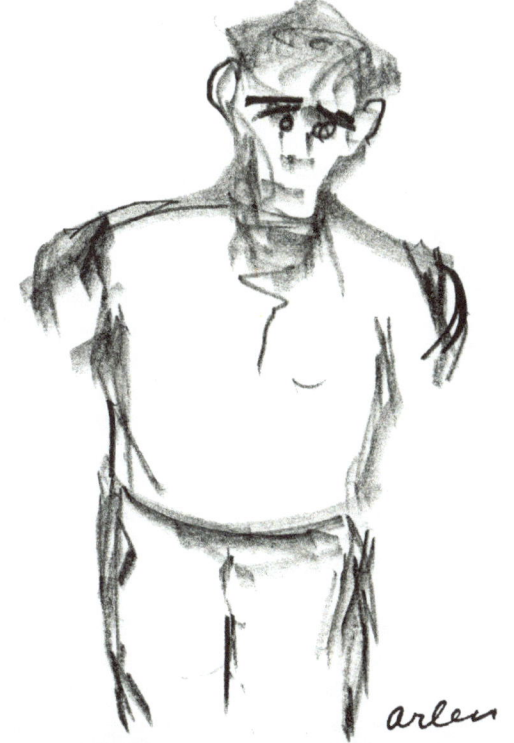

arlen

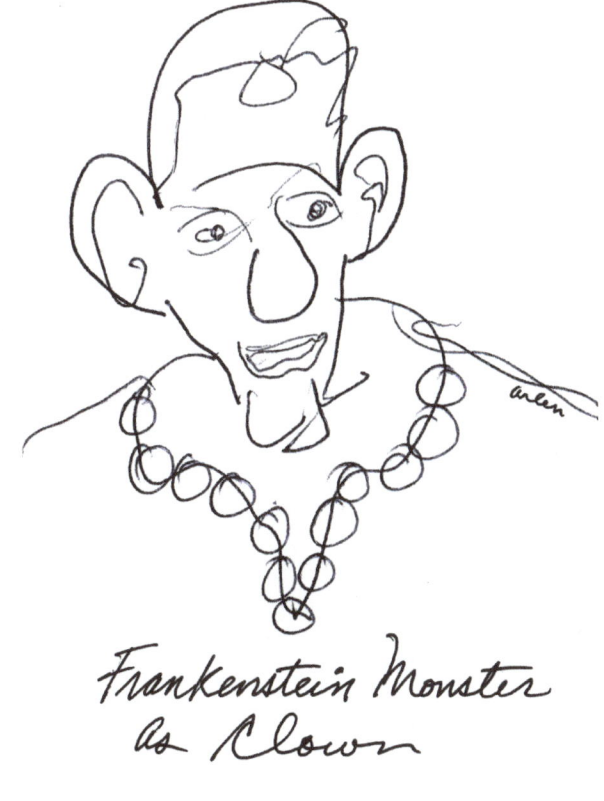

arlen

Frankenstein Monster
as Clown

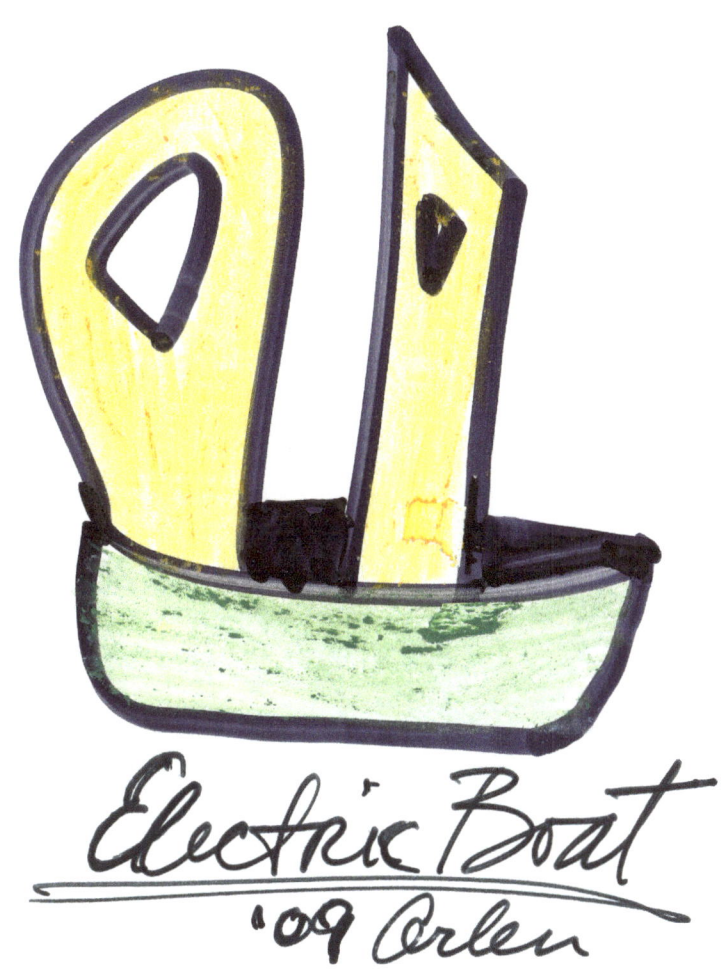

Electric Boat
'09 Arlen

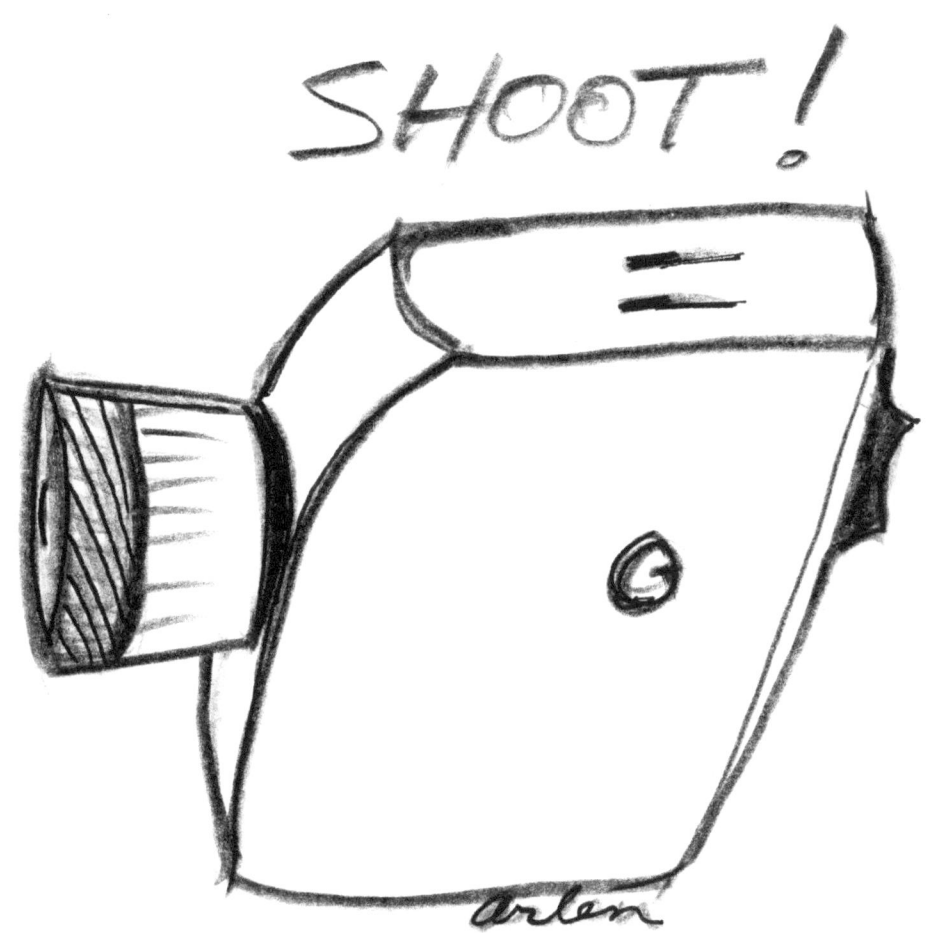

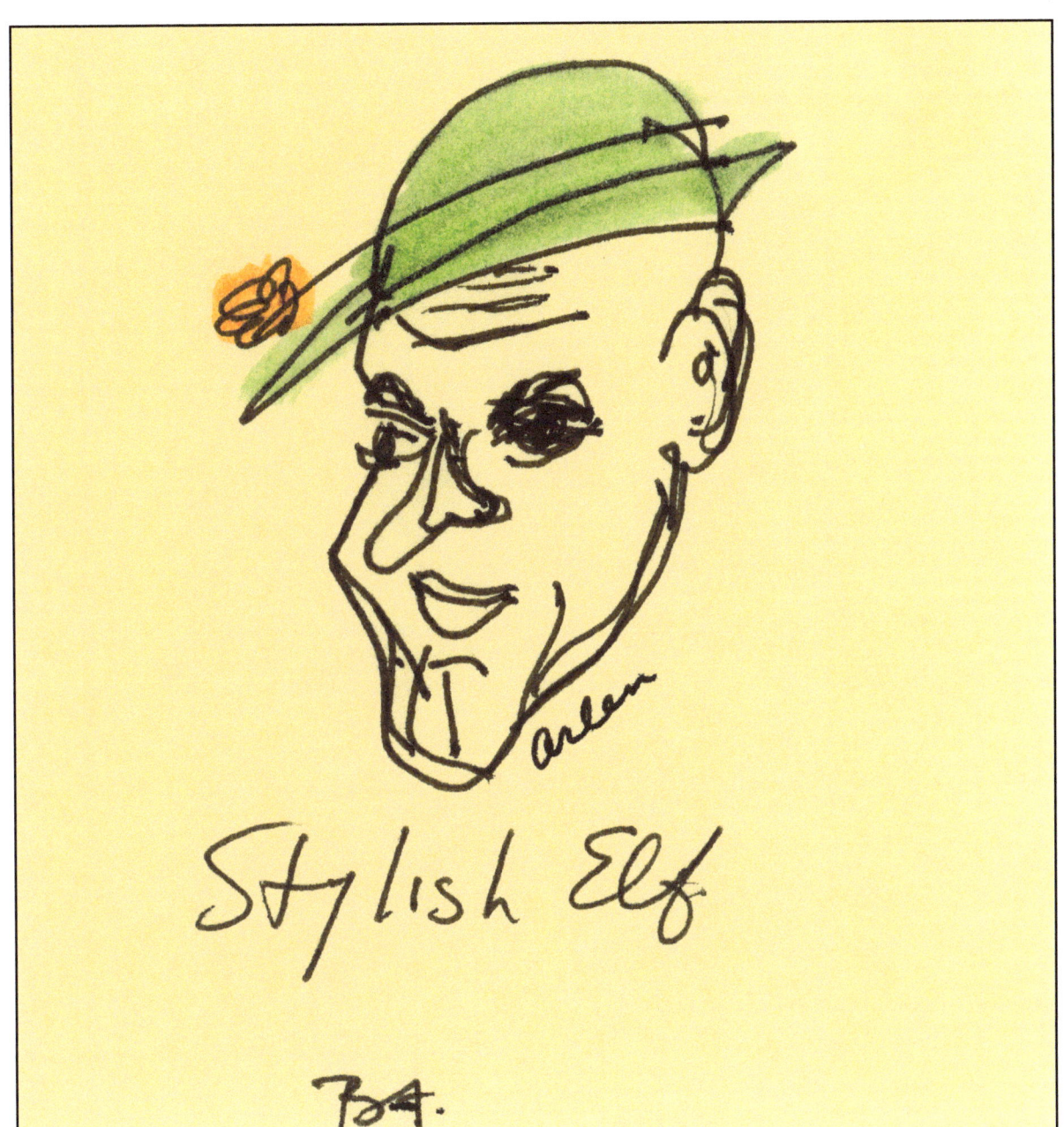

Stylish Elf

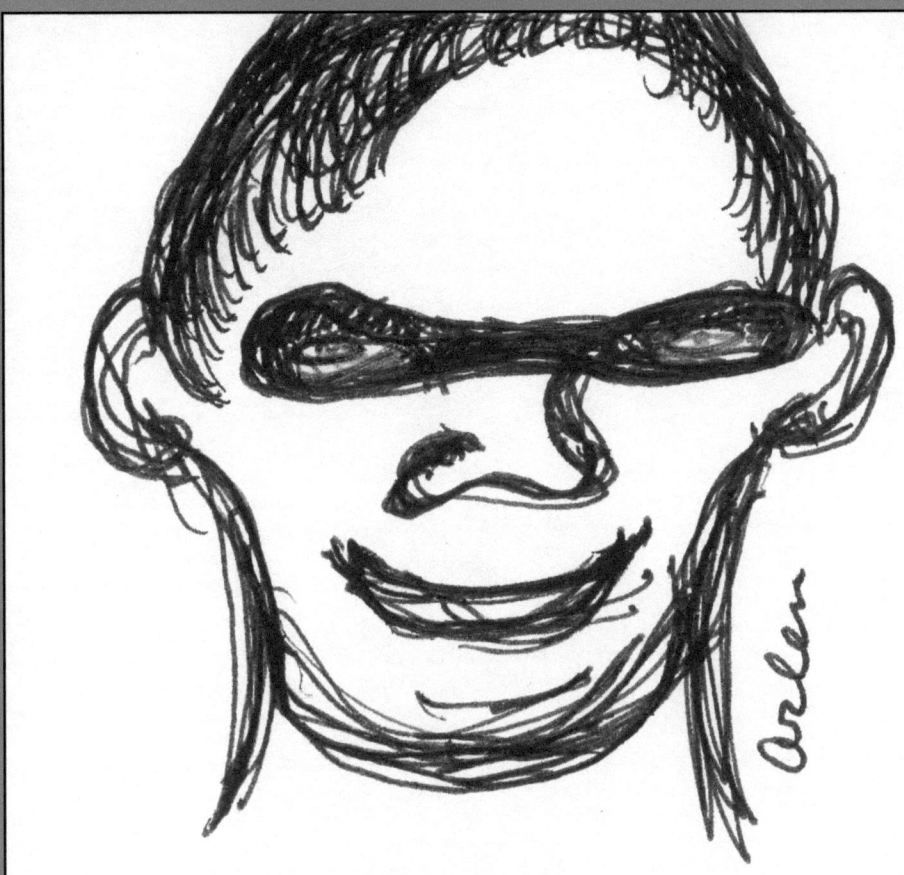

Bad Bat Boy

BATMAN'S
QUESTION
MARK

Arlen

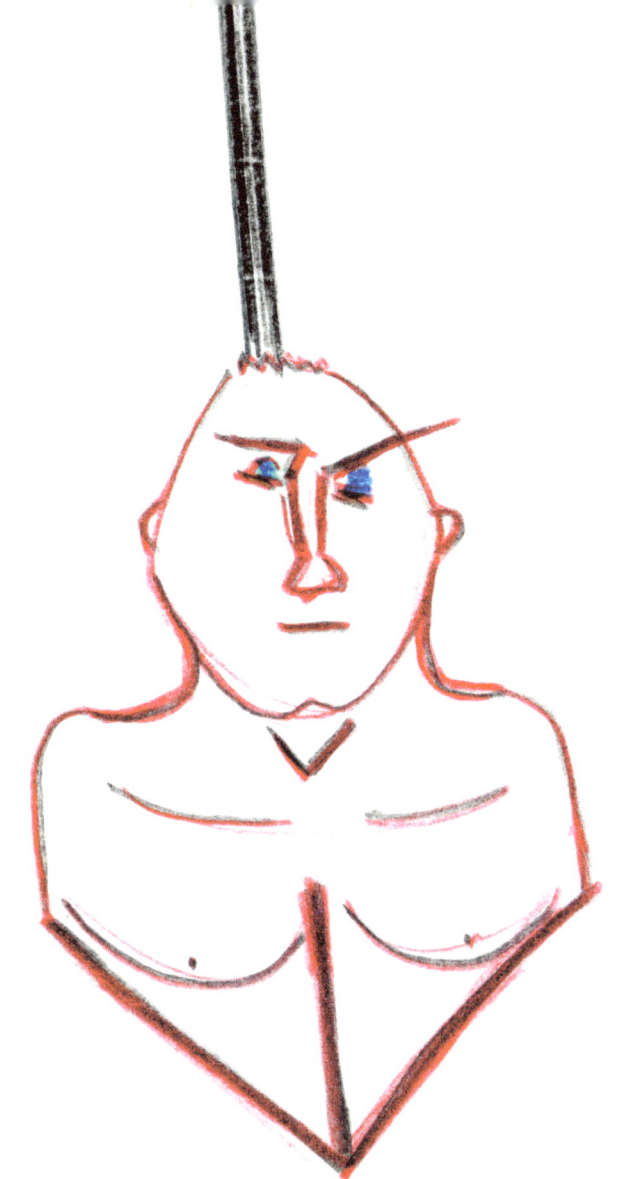

ARROW HEAD
allen '09

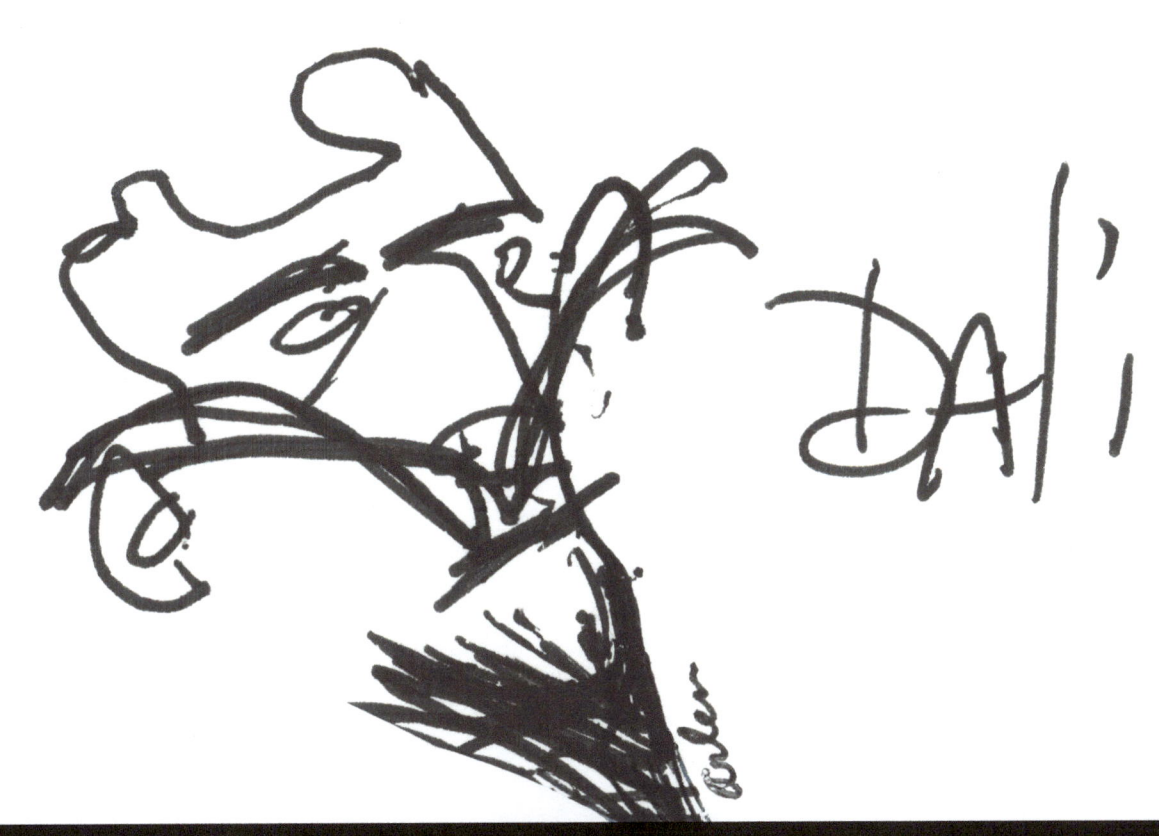

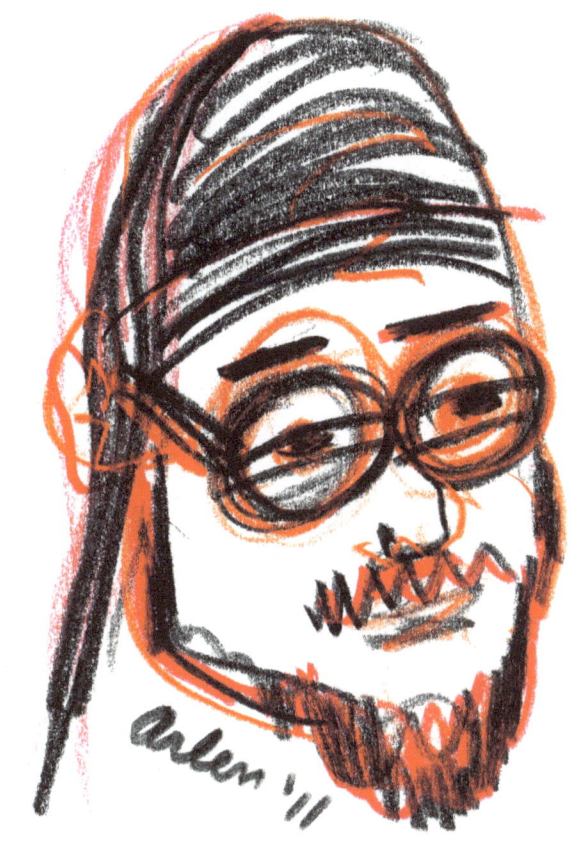

ART PROFESSOR

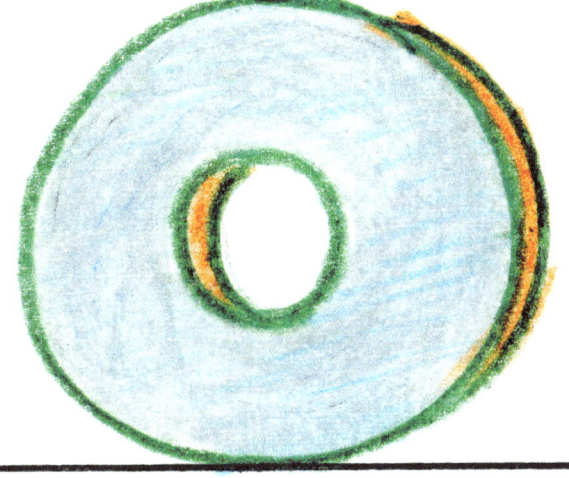

ORIGINAL Wheel
- areen

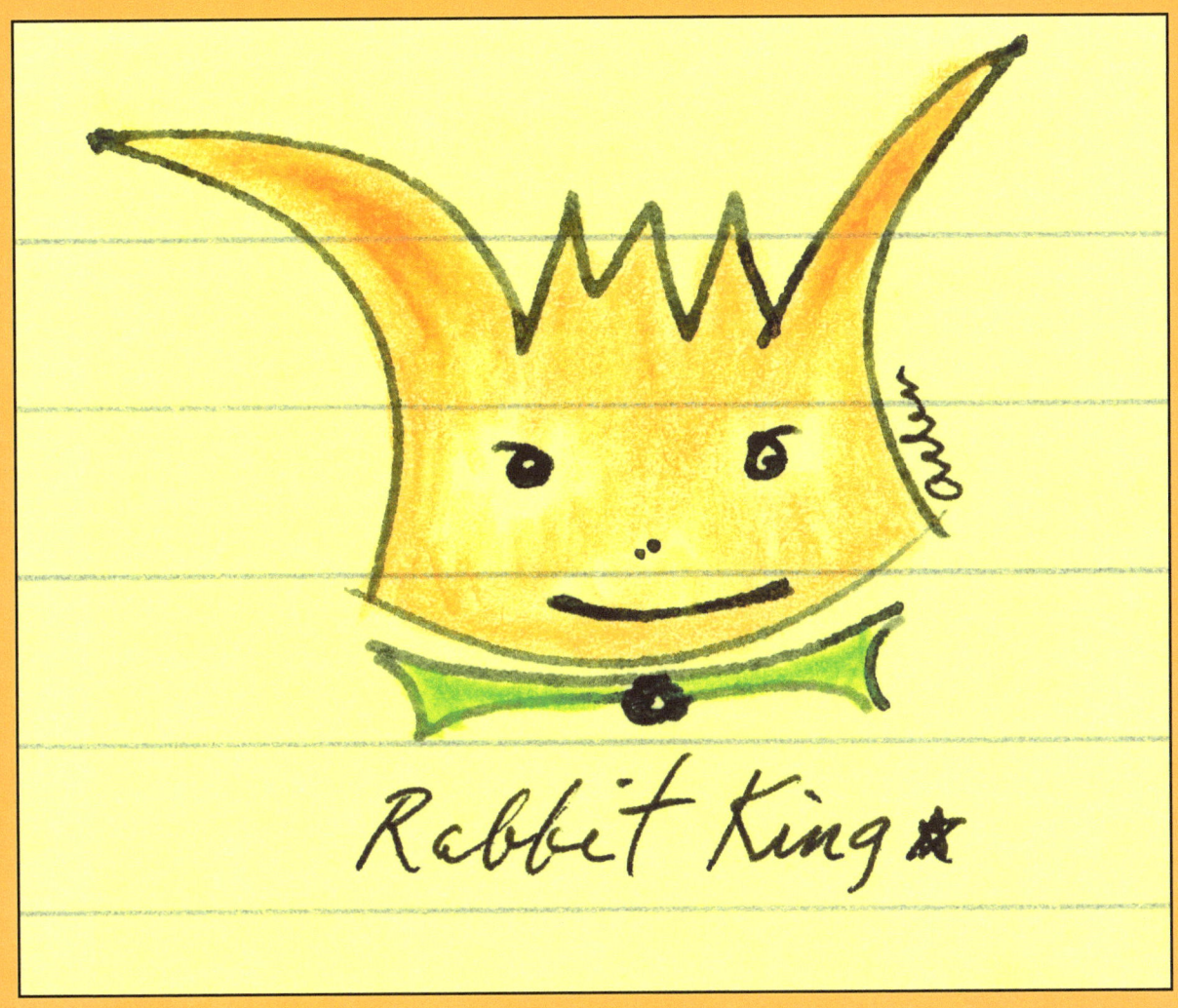

Rabbit King*

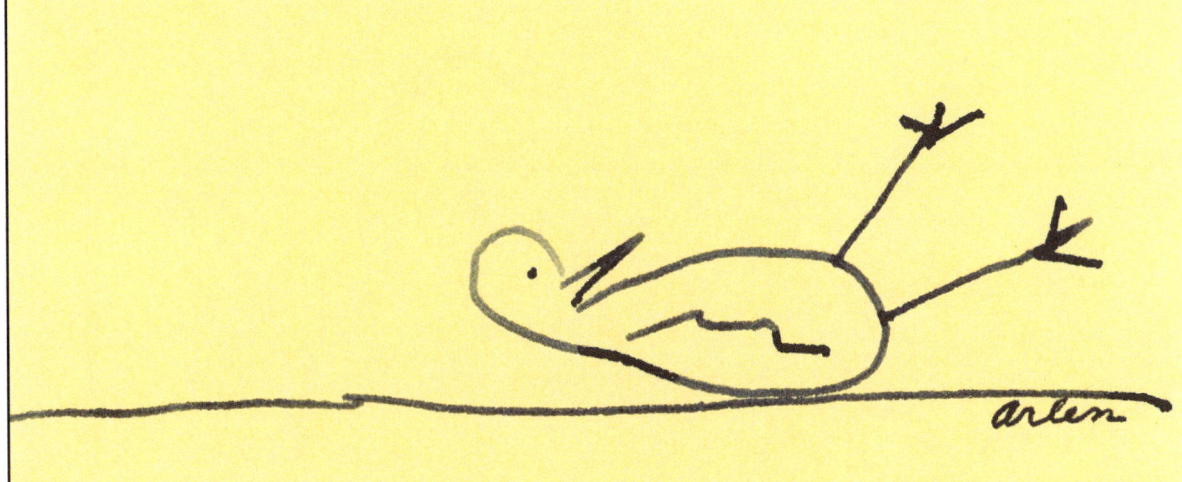

Avian Abs Workout?

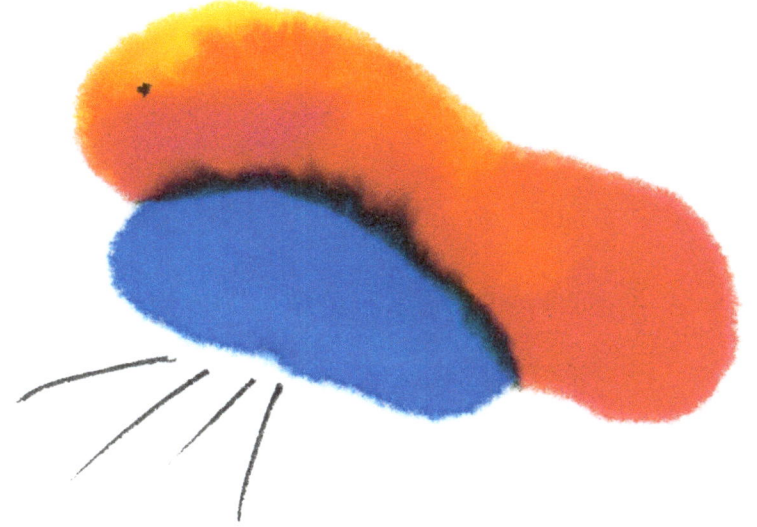

MR. WORM TAKES
A MAGIC PILLOW RIDE

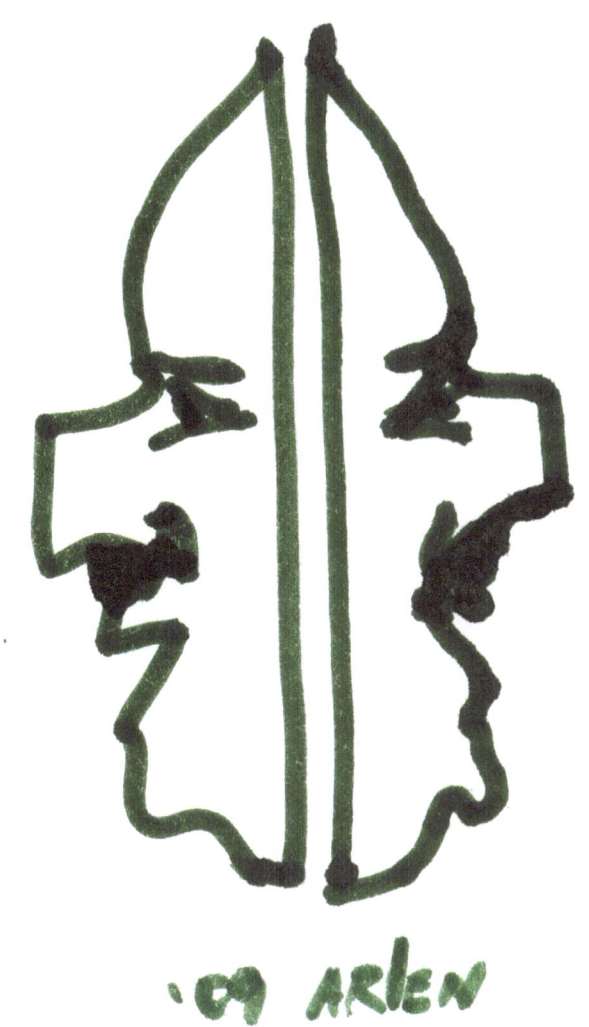

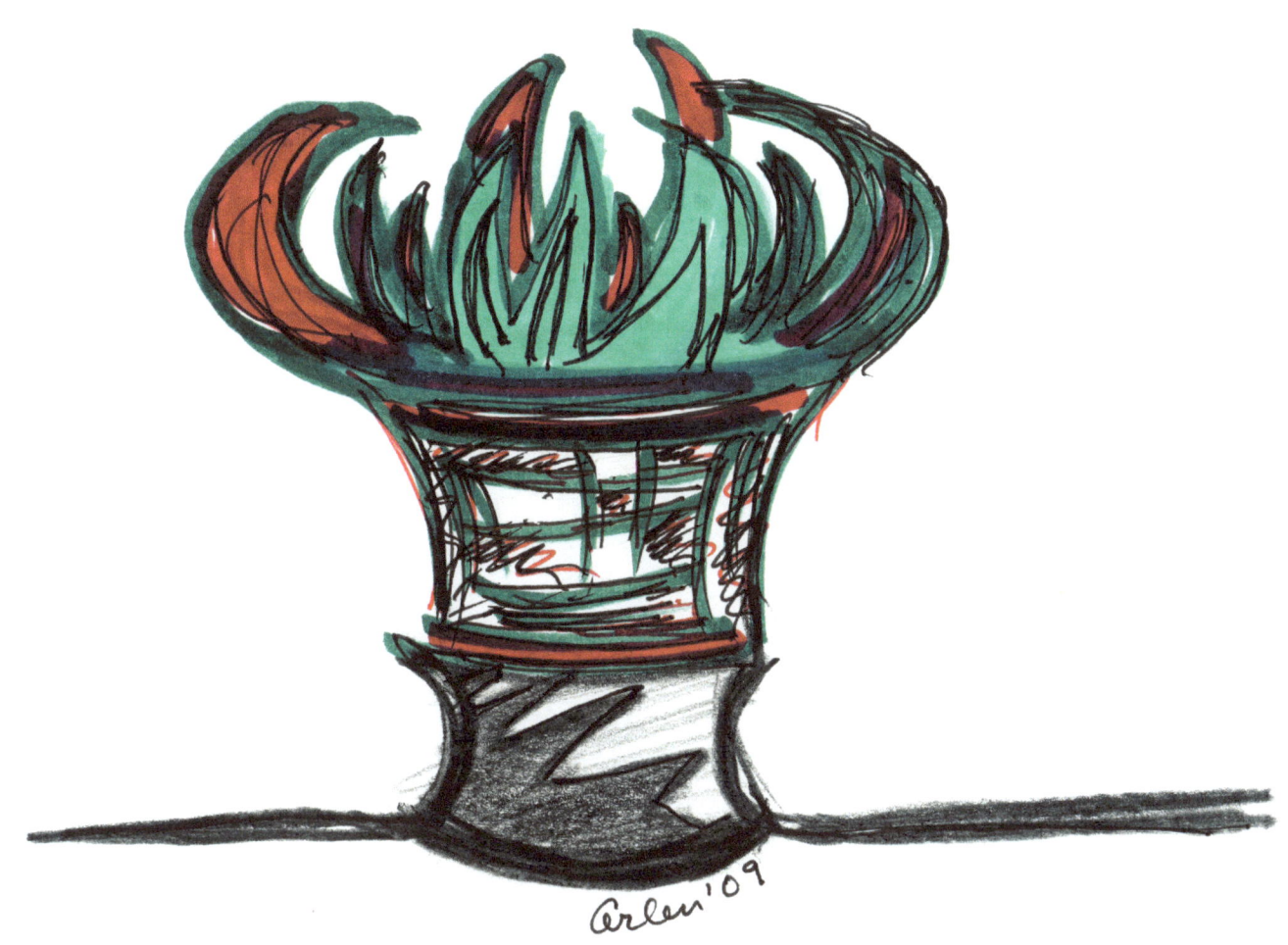

Arlen '09

Evil Roof Exhaust

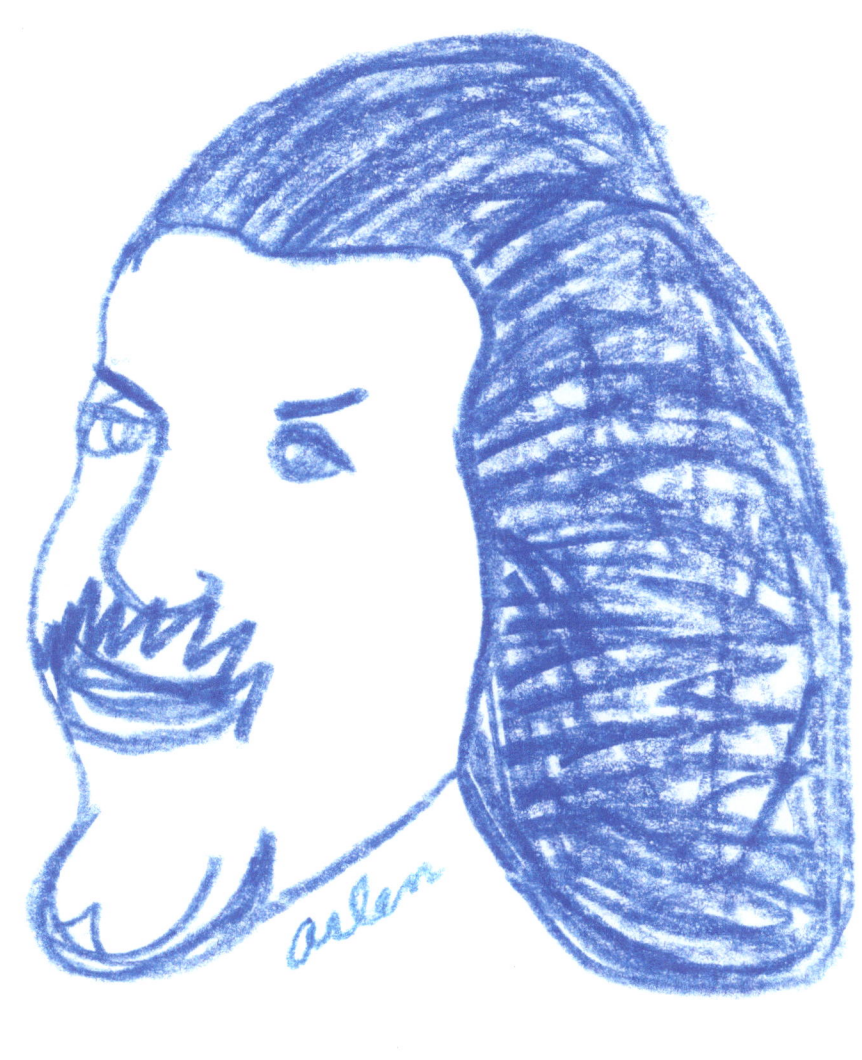

Will.

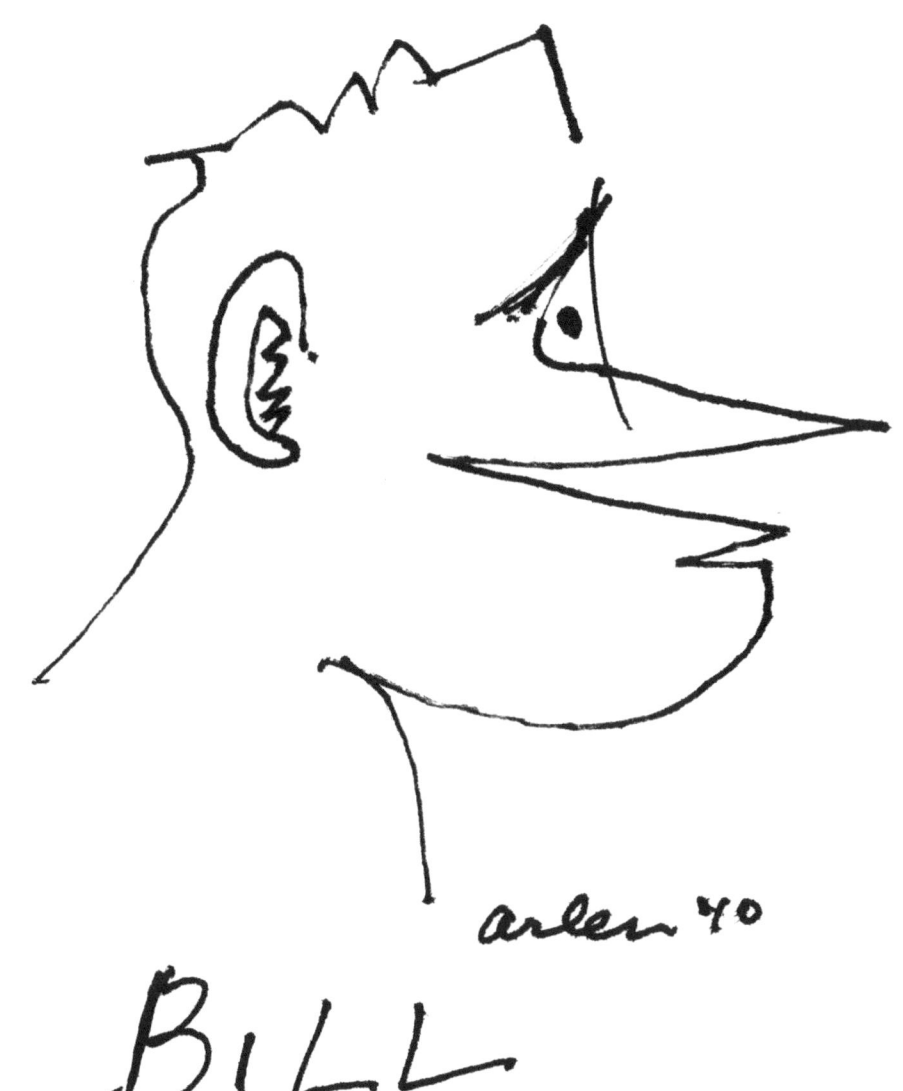

BILL

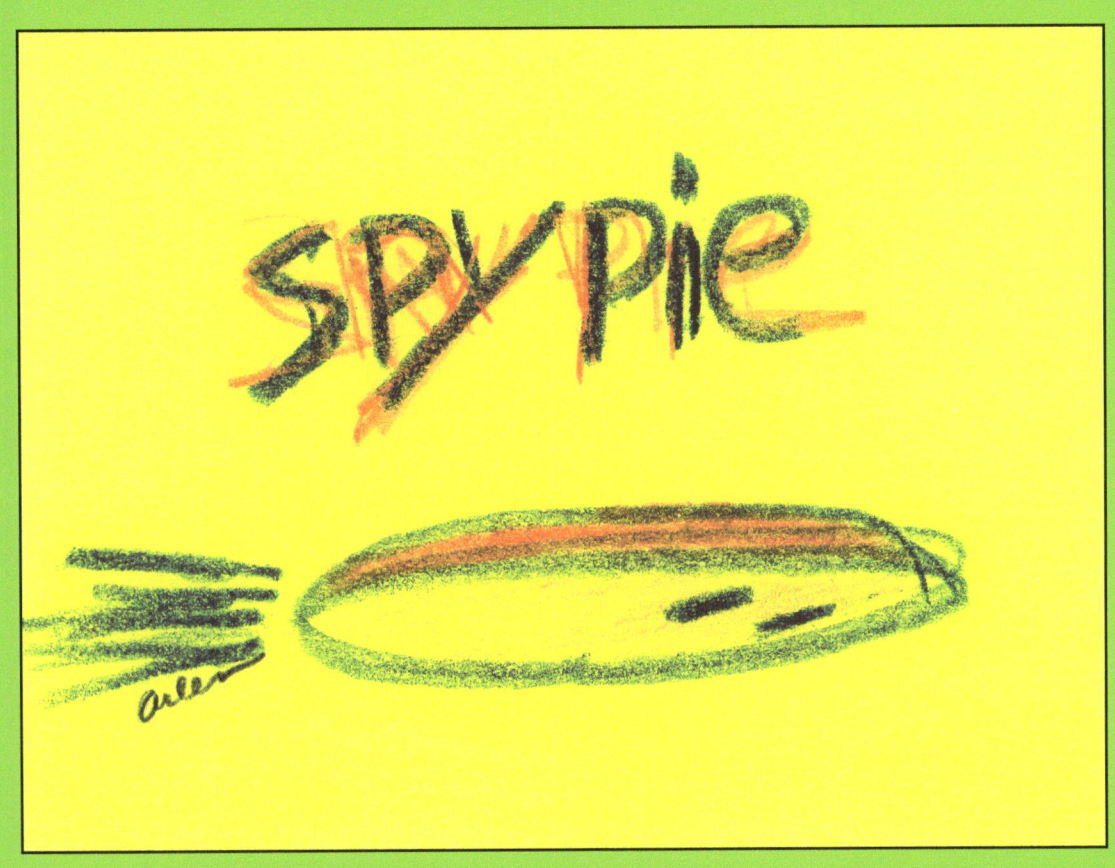

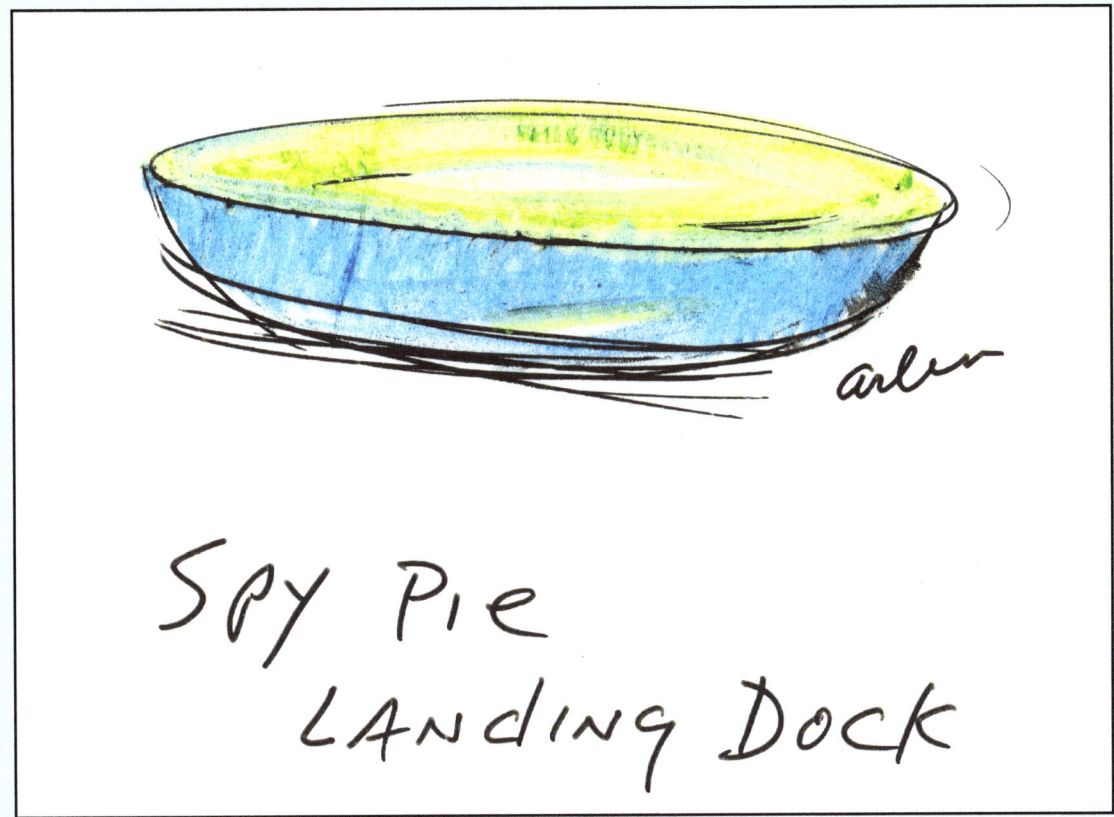

Spy Pie
Landing Dock

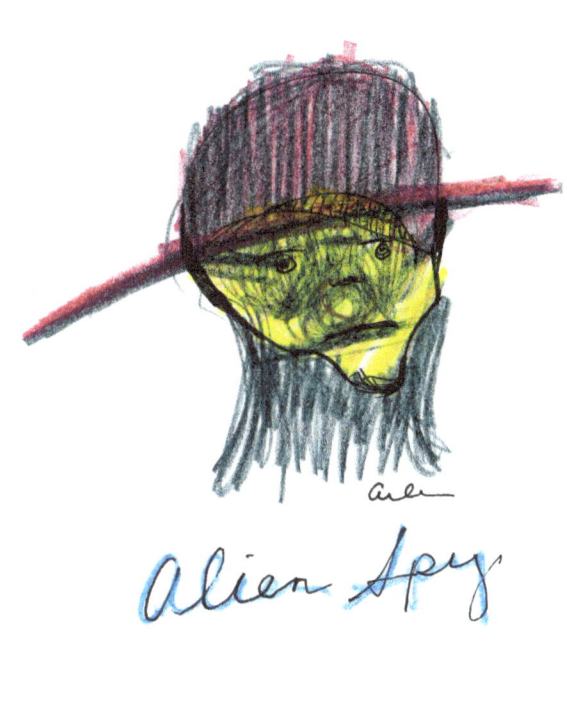

Alien Spy

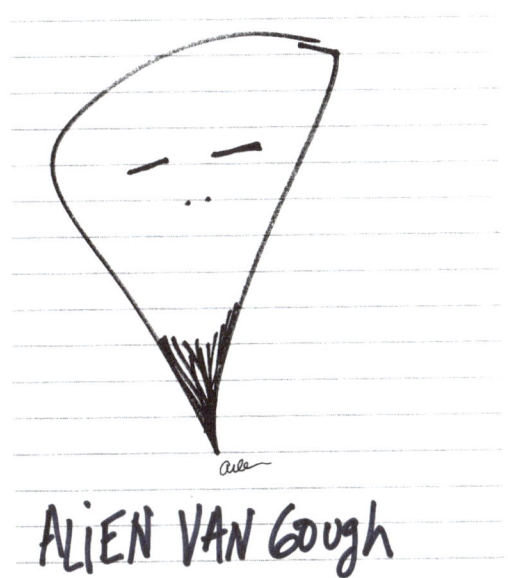

ALIEN VAN GOUGH

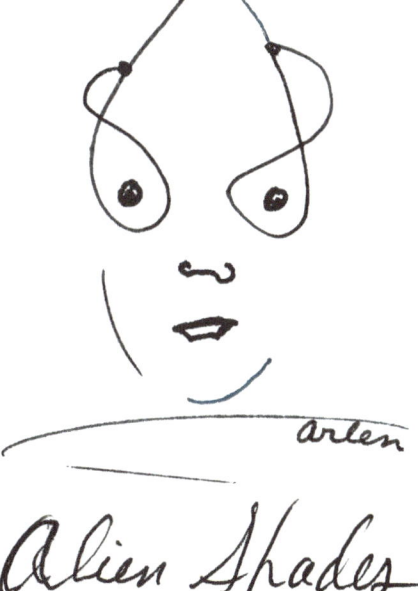

Alien Shades

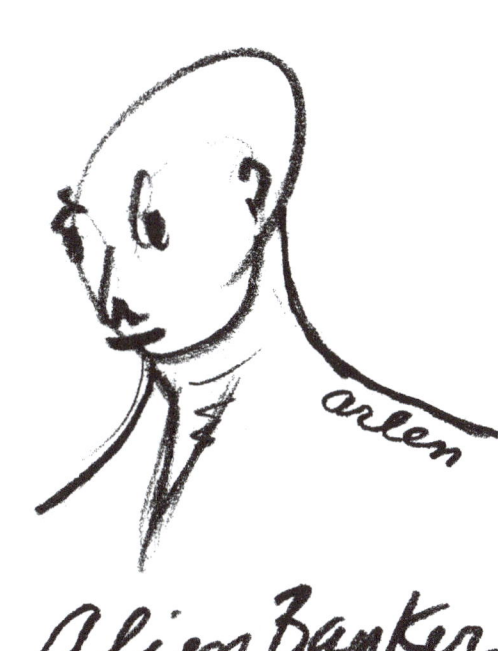

Alien Banker

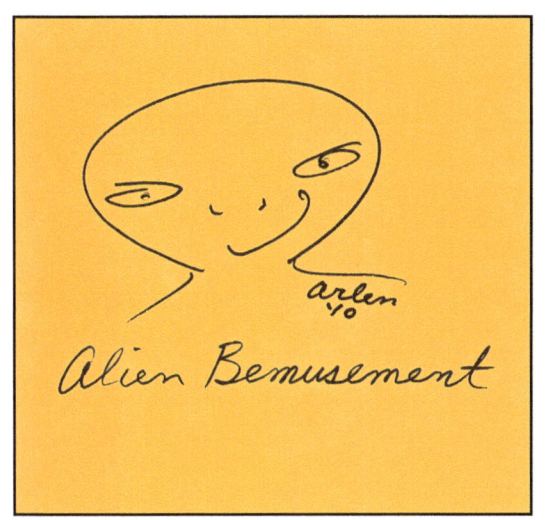

Alien Bemusement

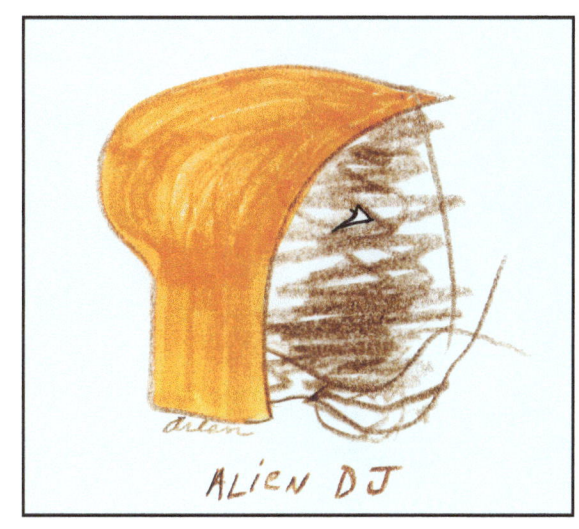

ALIEN DJ

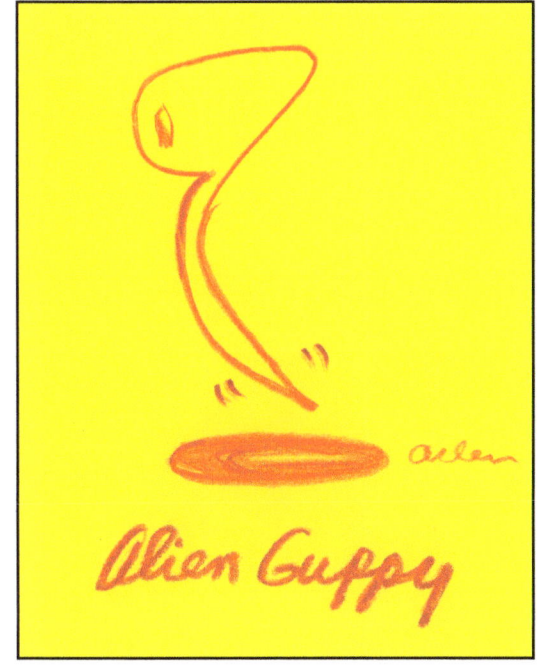

Alien Guppy

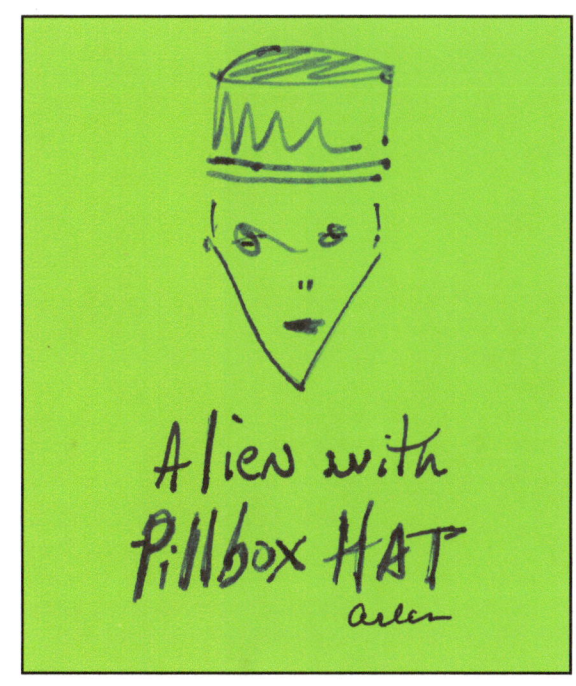

Alien with Pillbox HAT

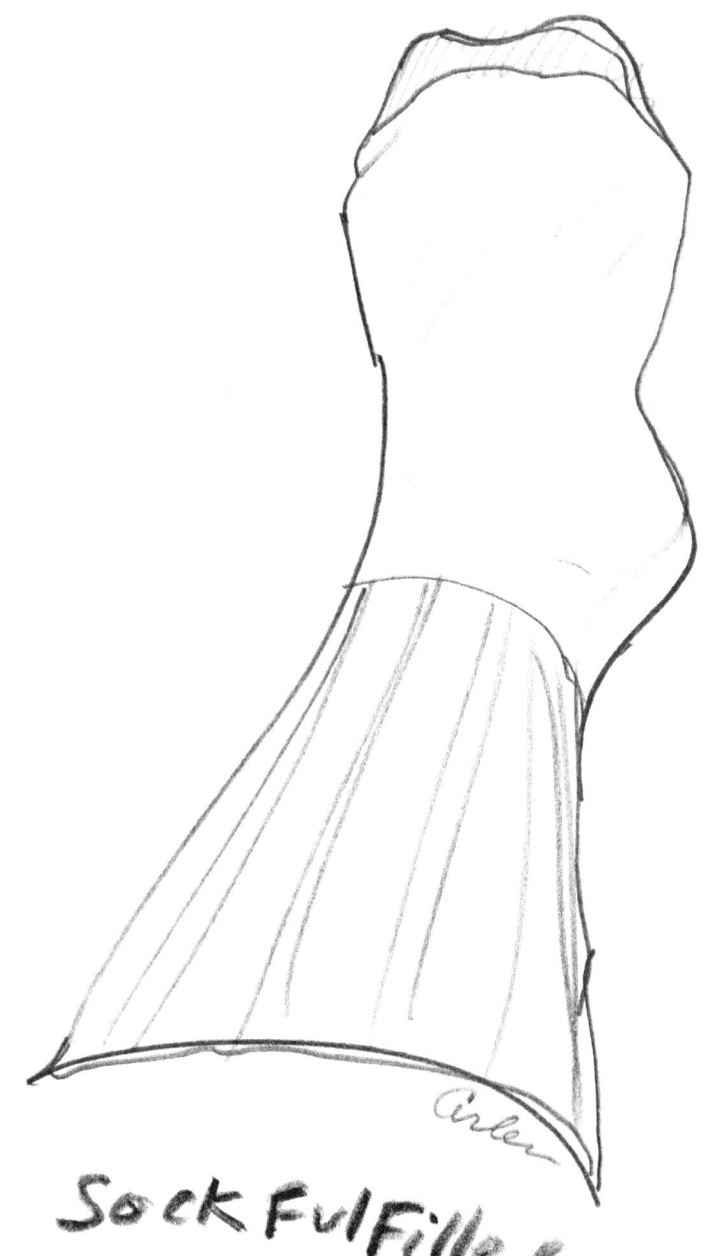

Sock Fulfilled

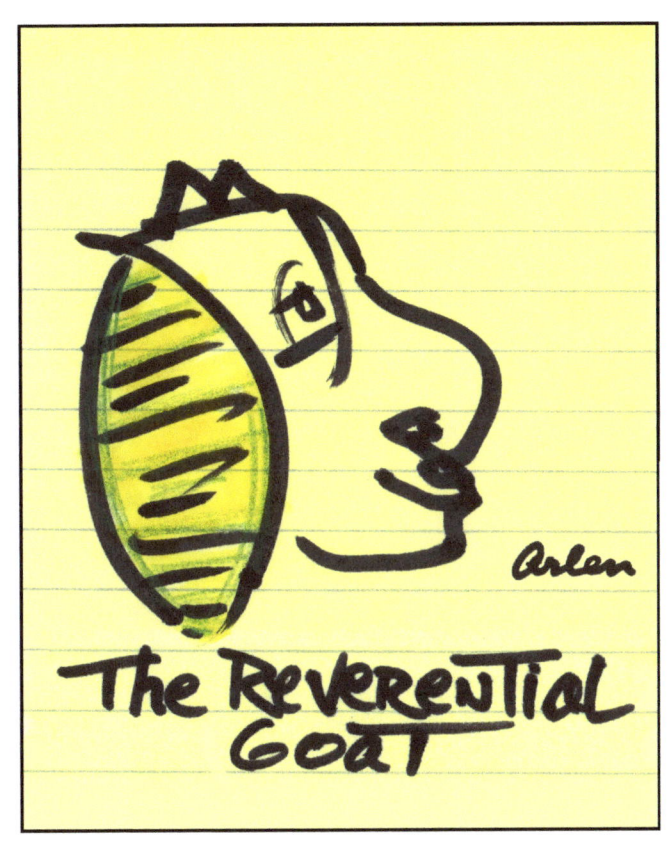

The Reverential Goat

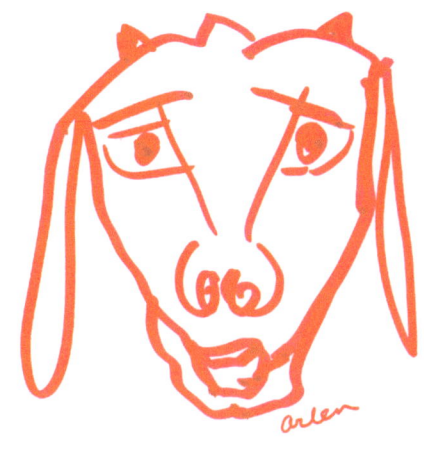

WHY IS THIS GOAT WORRIED?

Chicken Noodle

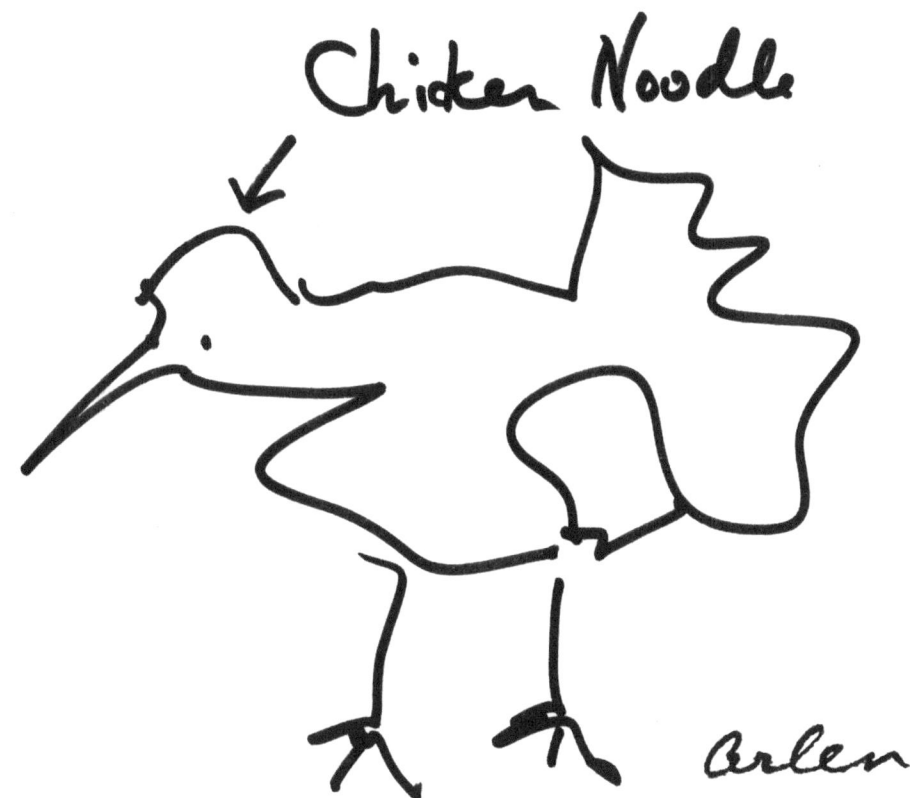

arlen

NOG OF THE EGG

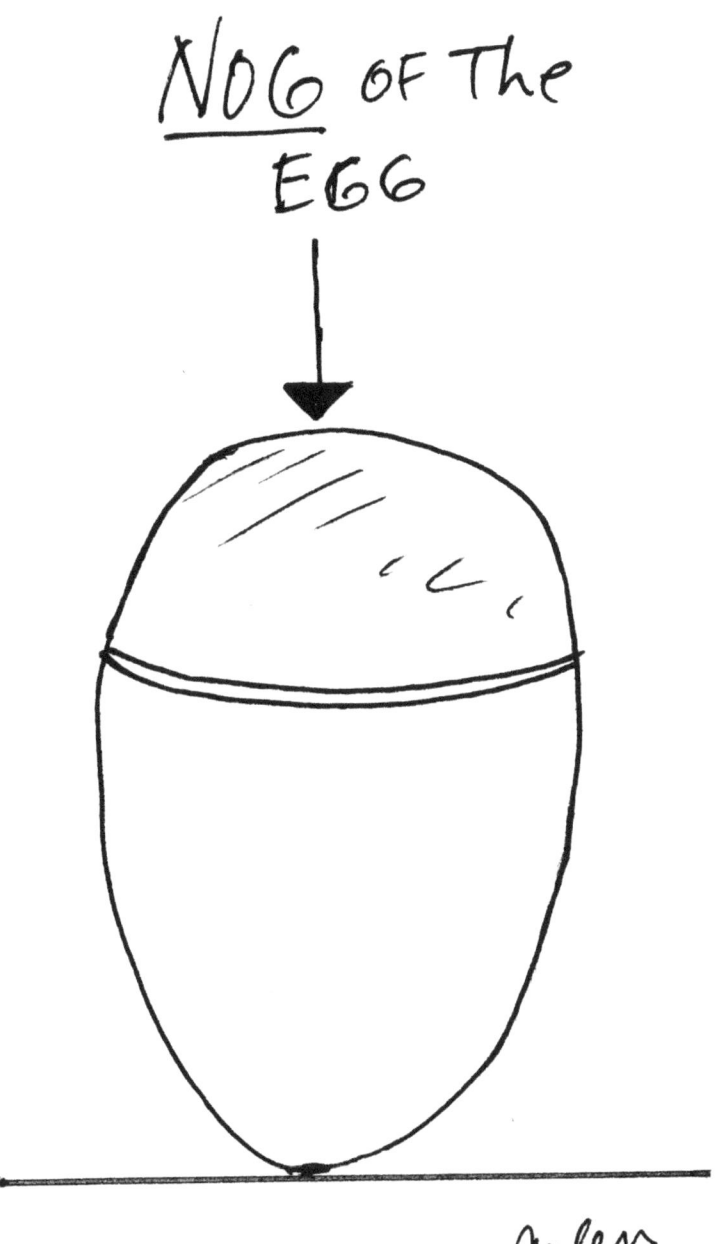

arlen

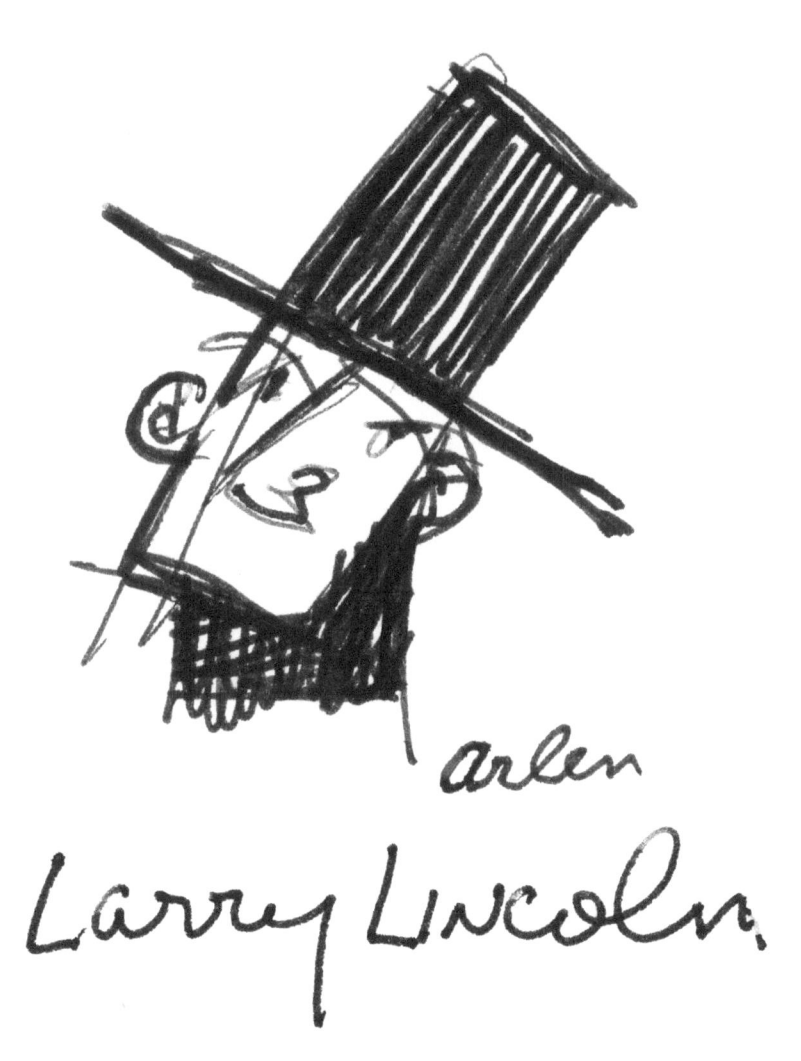

arlen

Larry Lincoln.

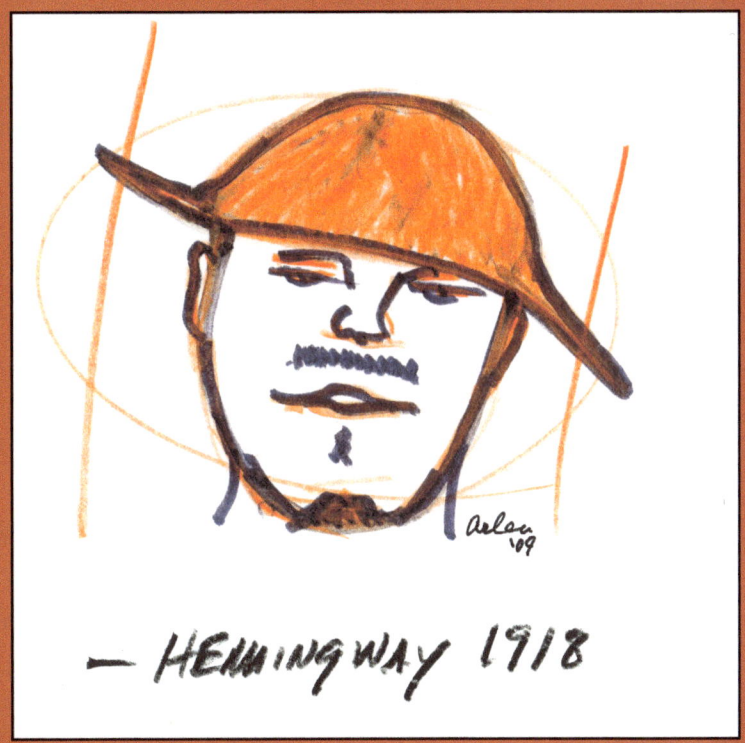

— HEMINGWAY 1918

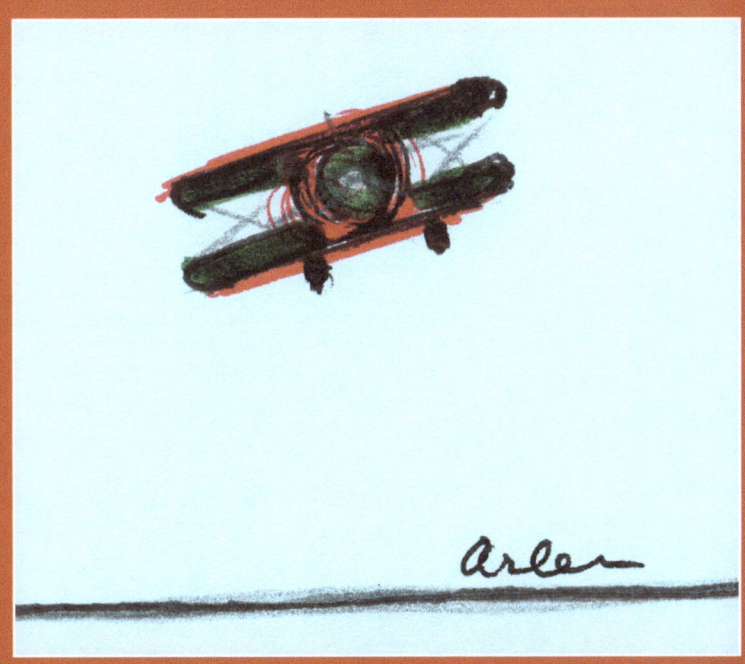

DAVEY CROCKETTS'
NEW
PLAID SKIN
CAP.

arlen

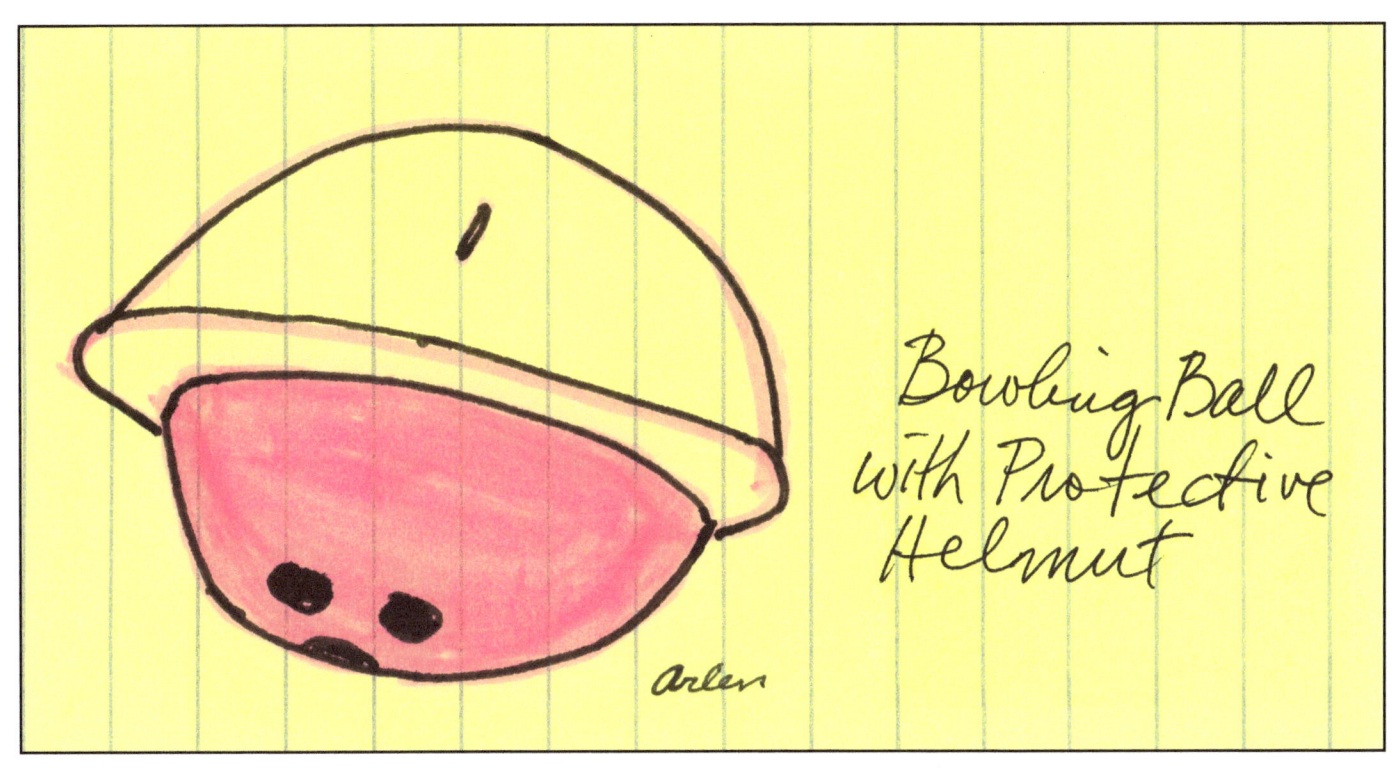

Bowling Ball with Protective Helmut

arlen

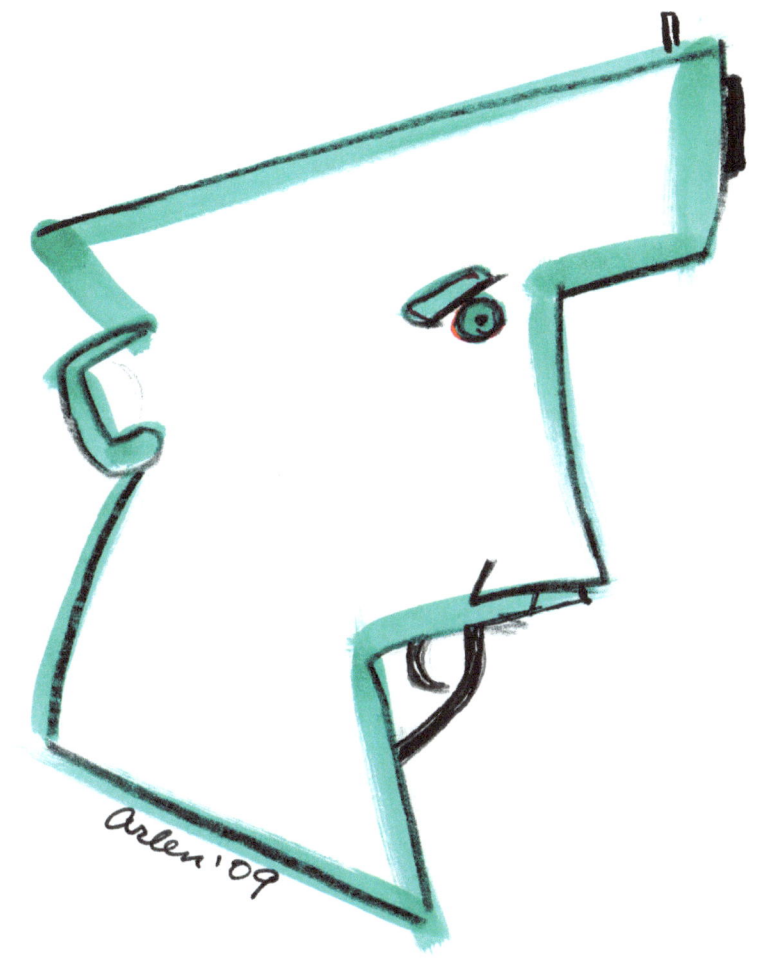

Arlen '09

Gunman

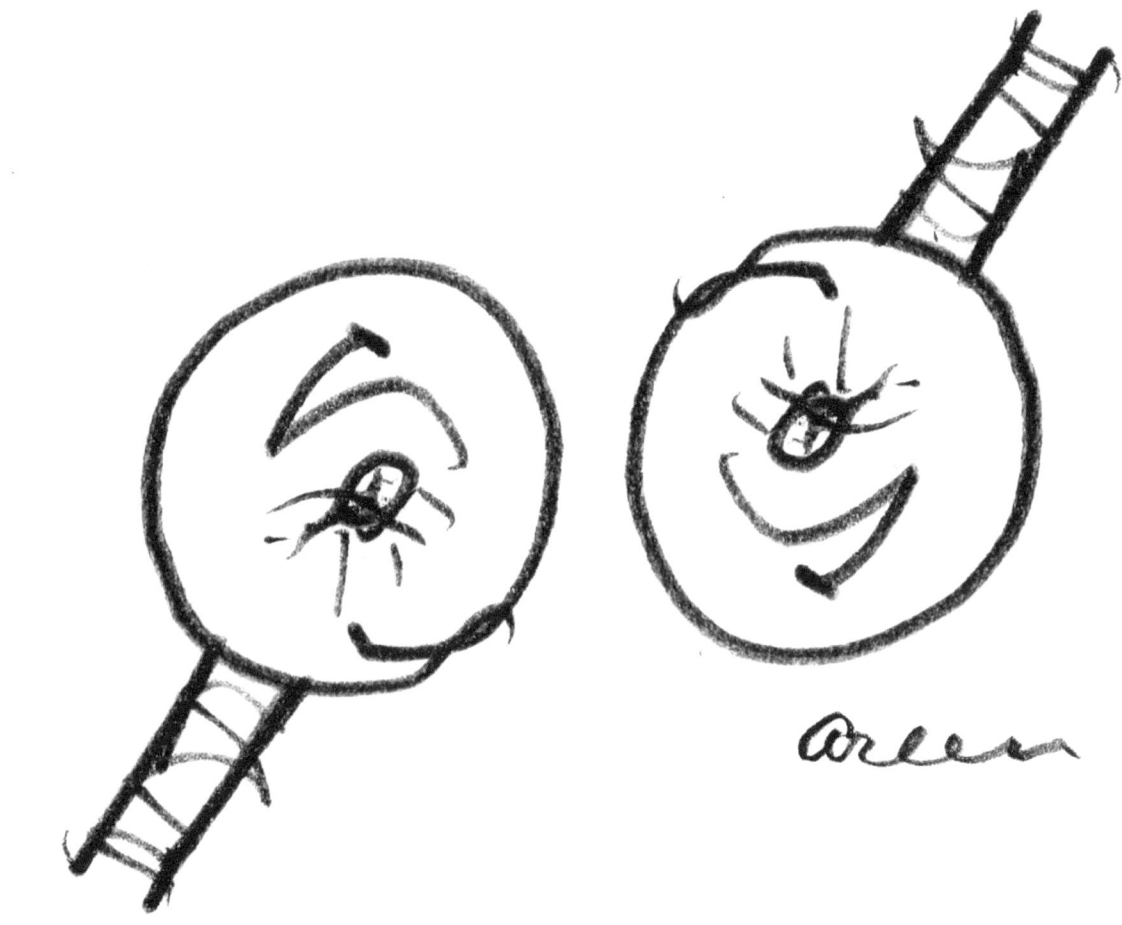

Bernie & Frieda

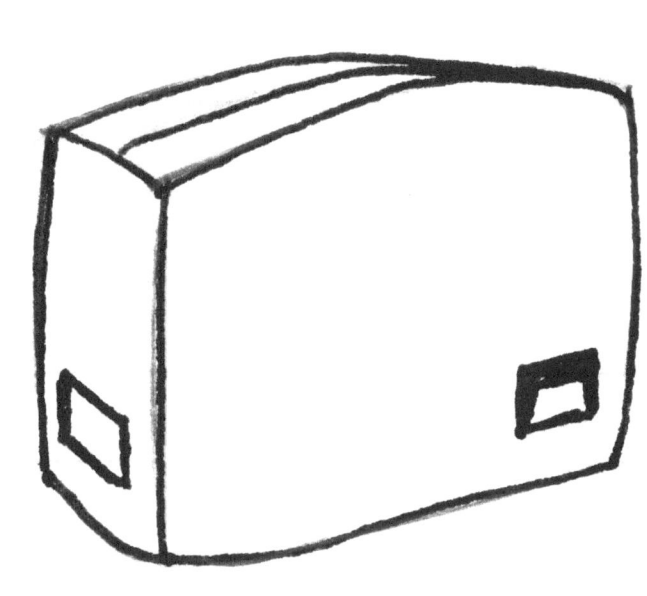

THE UNKNOWN TOASTER
arlen '09

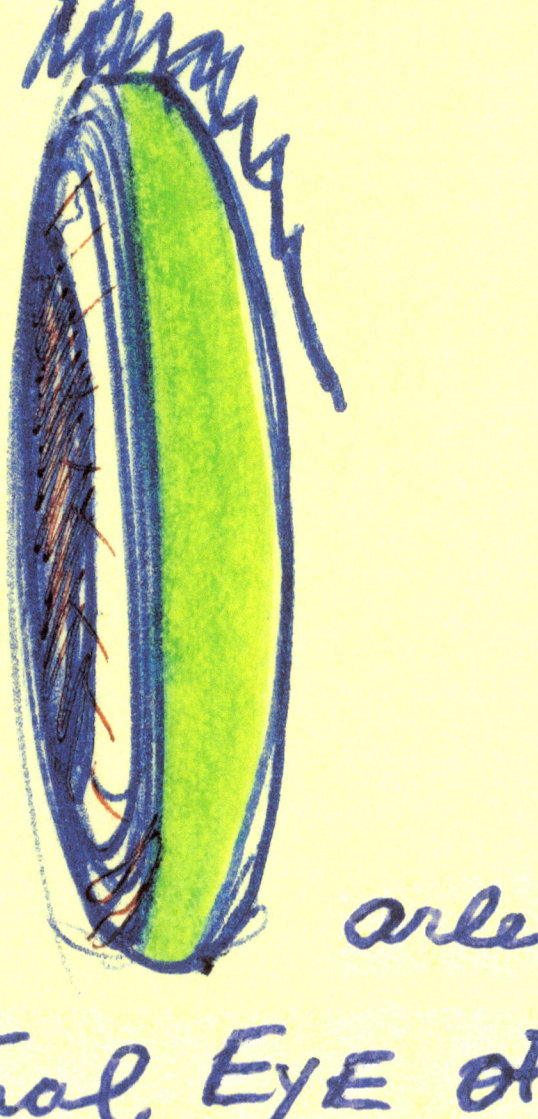

arlen

ActuaL EyE oF
THE
Beholder

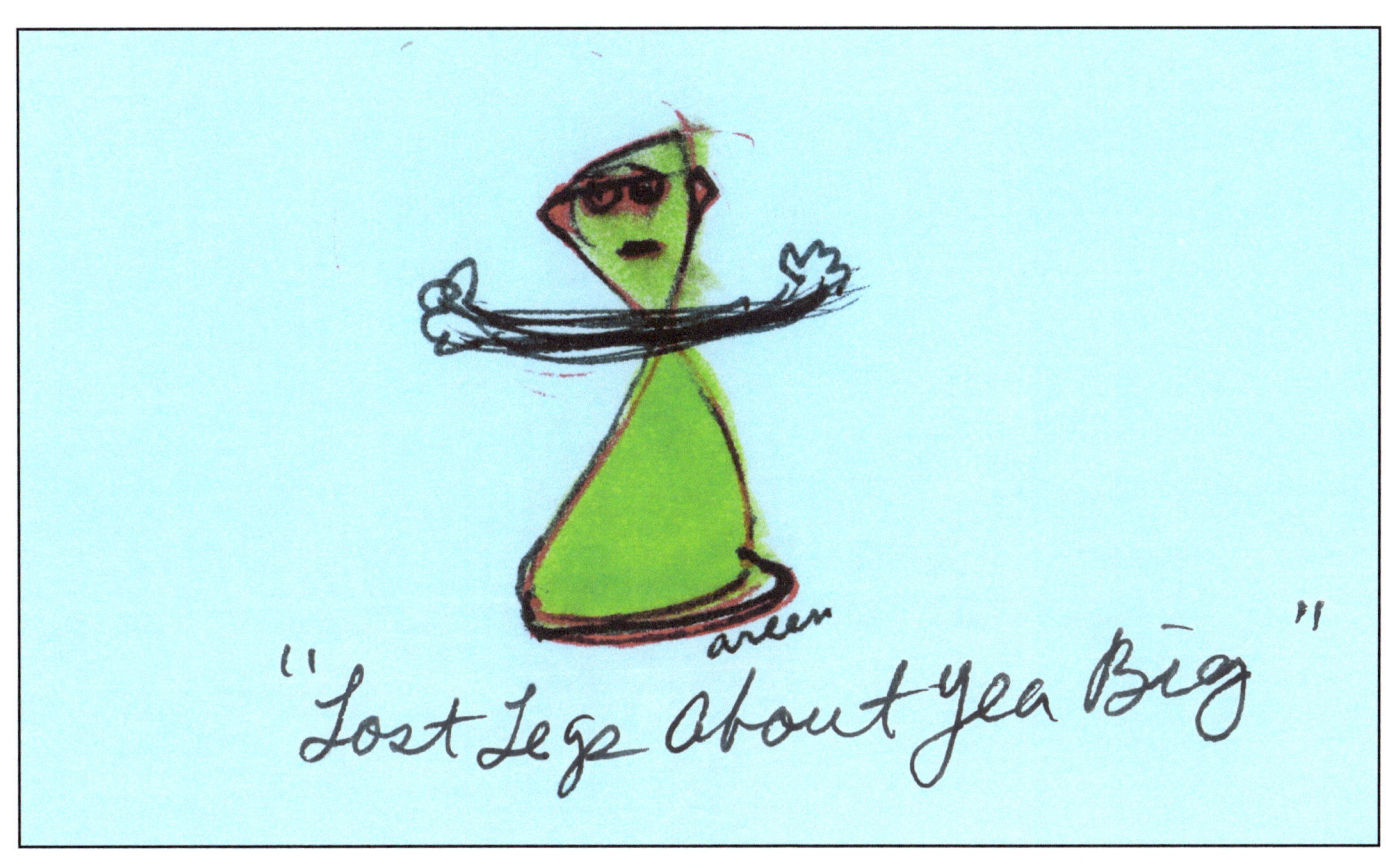

"Lost Legs about yea Big"

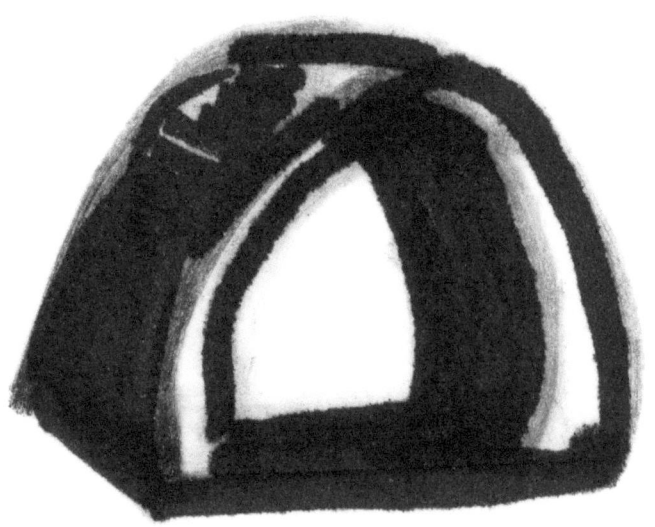

FREE Standing Tunnel

Allen '08

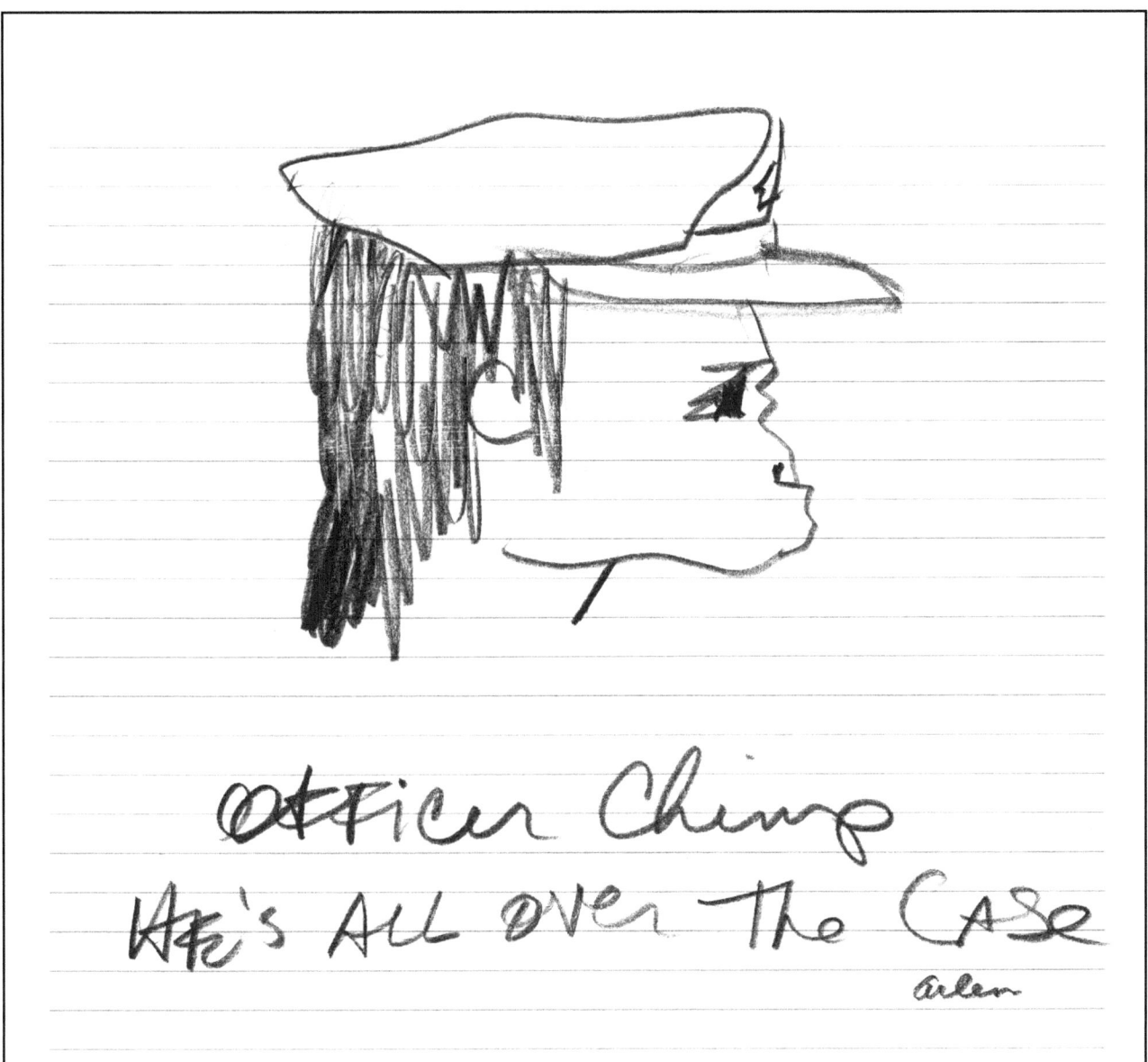

Officer Chimp
He's all over the case

arlen

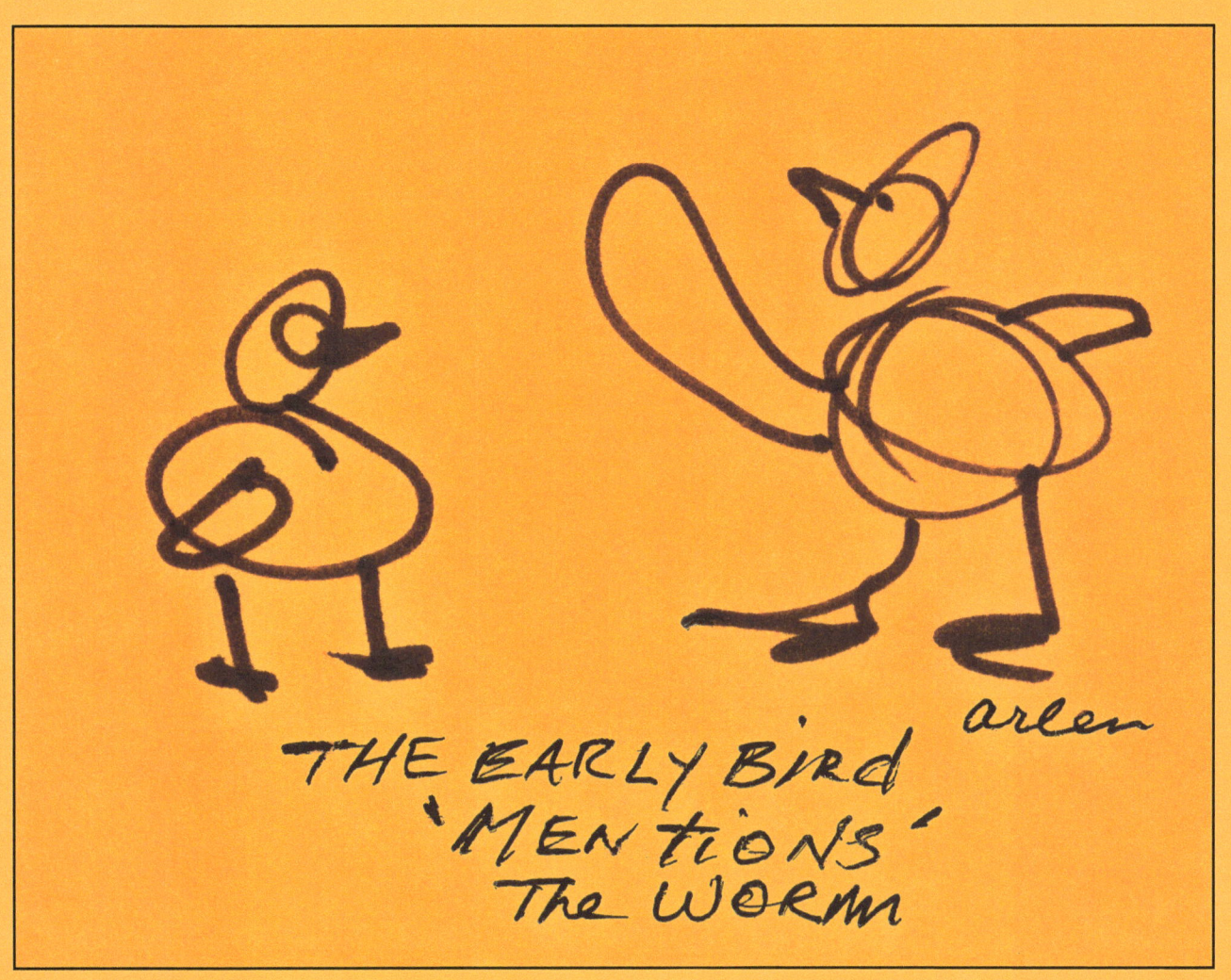

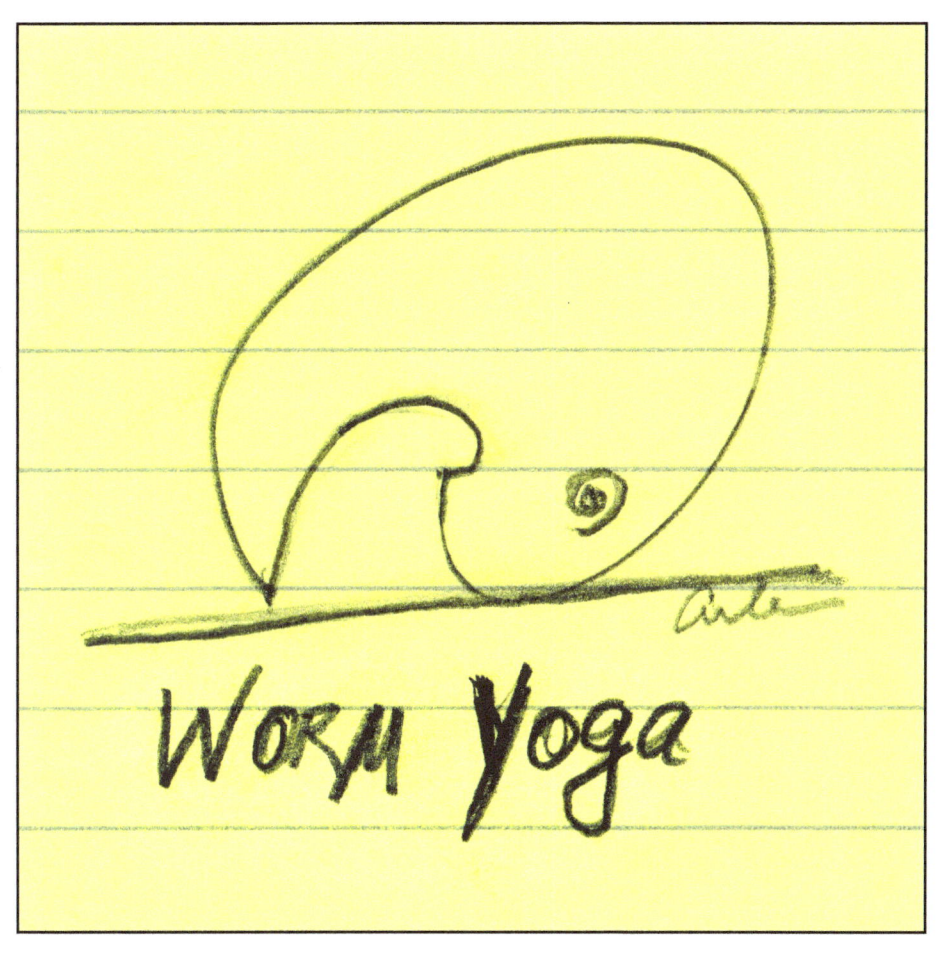

Worm Yoga

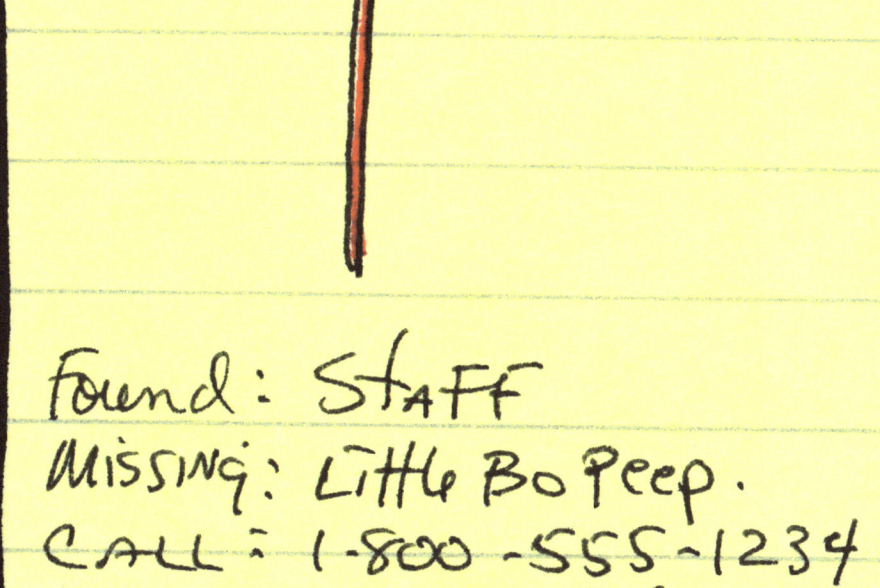

Found: STAFF
MISSING: Little Bo Peep.
CALL: 1-800-555-1234
allen

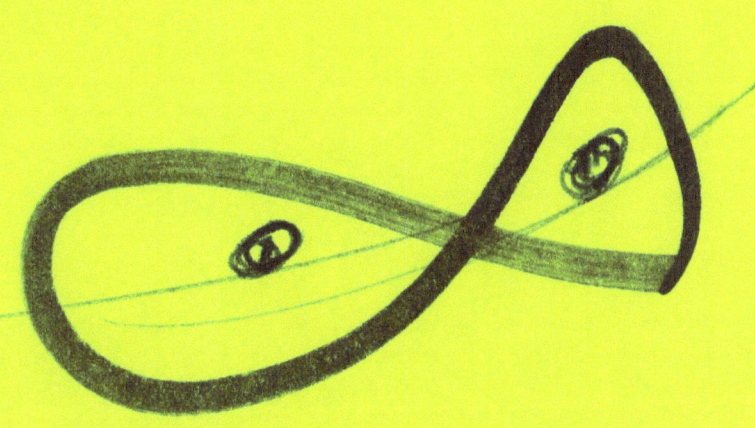

Rogue Hero
Mask

arlen

DANCING SCREW BALLET

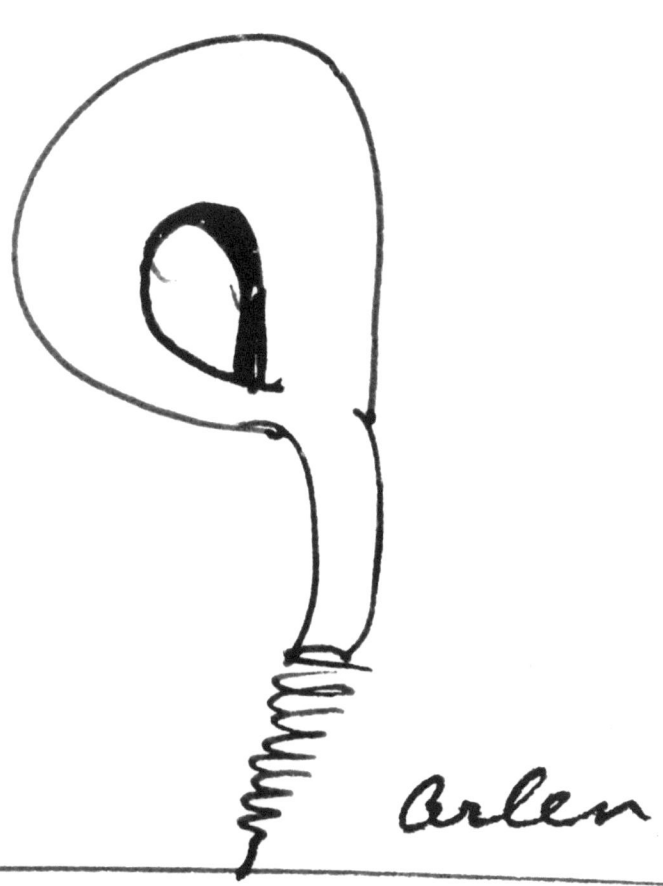

arlen

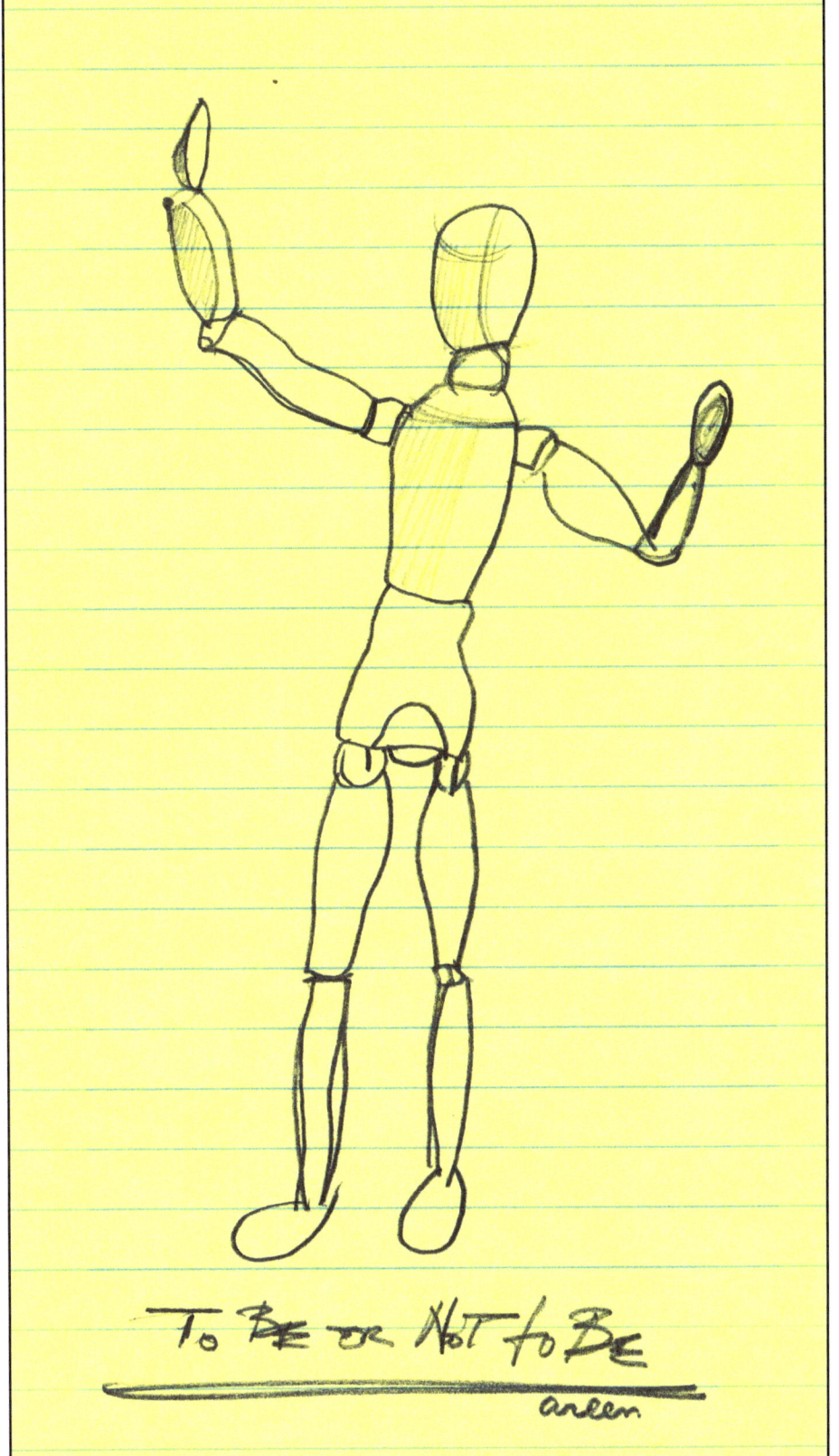

TO BE OR NOT TO BE

arlen

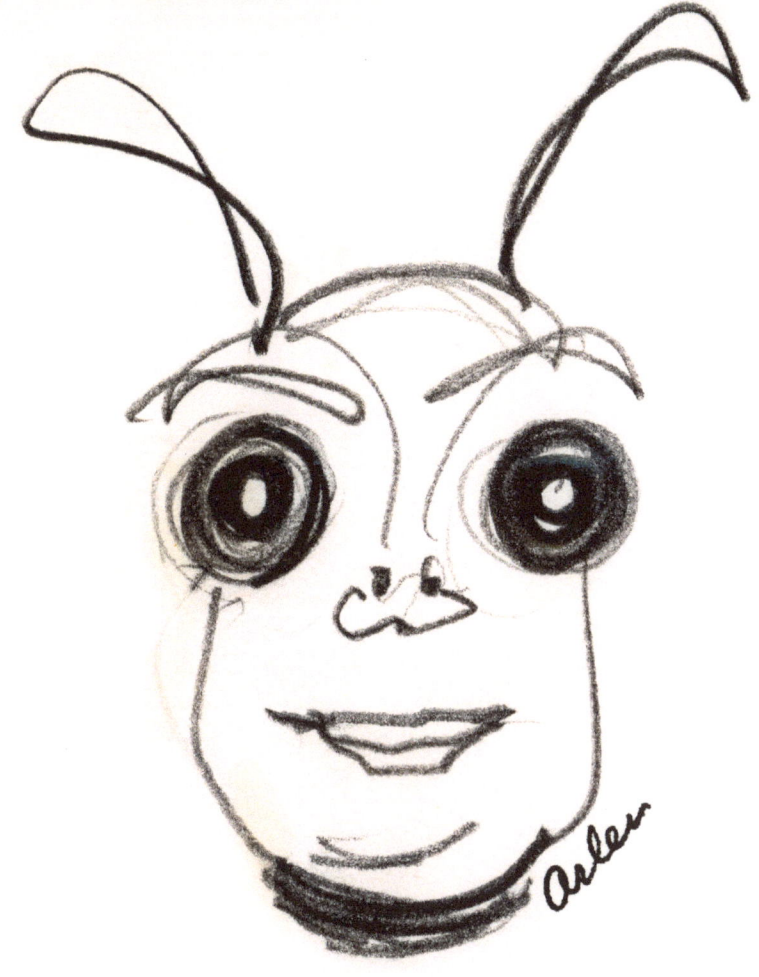

CRICKET MAN
WHAT A GENTLEMAN

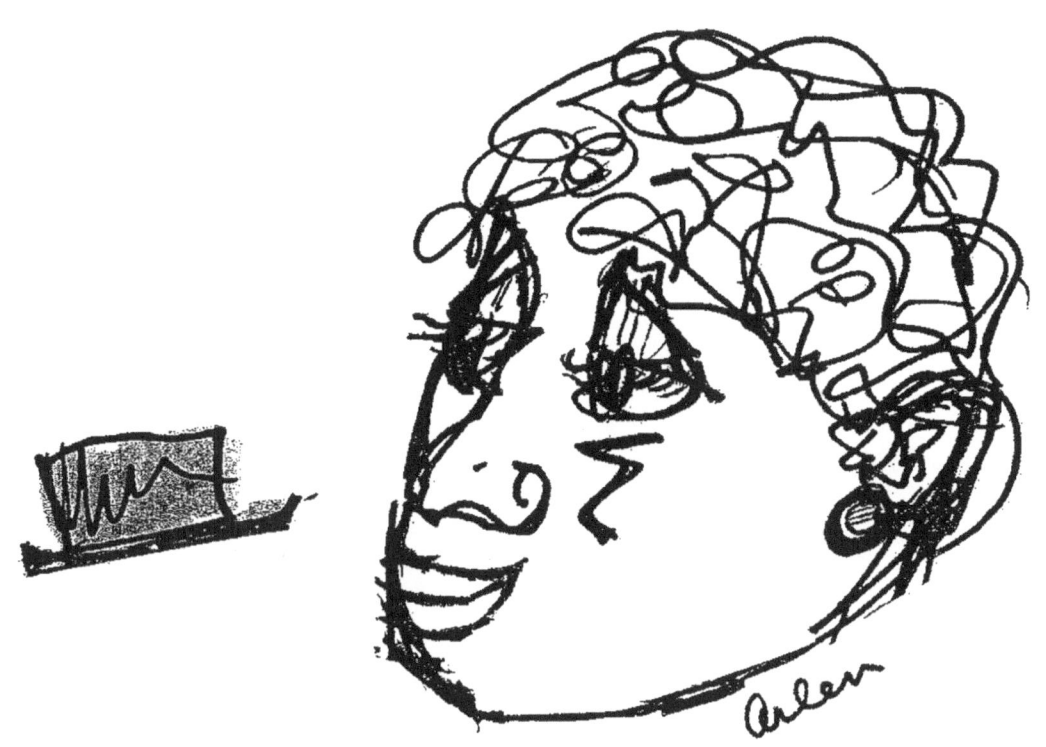

HARPO MARX'S
MOM

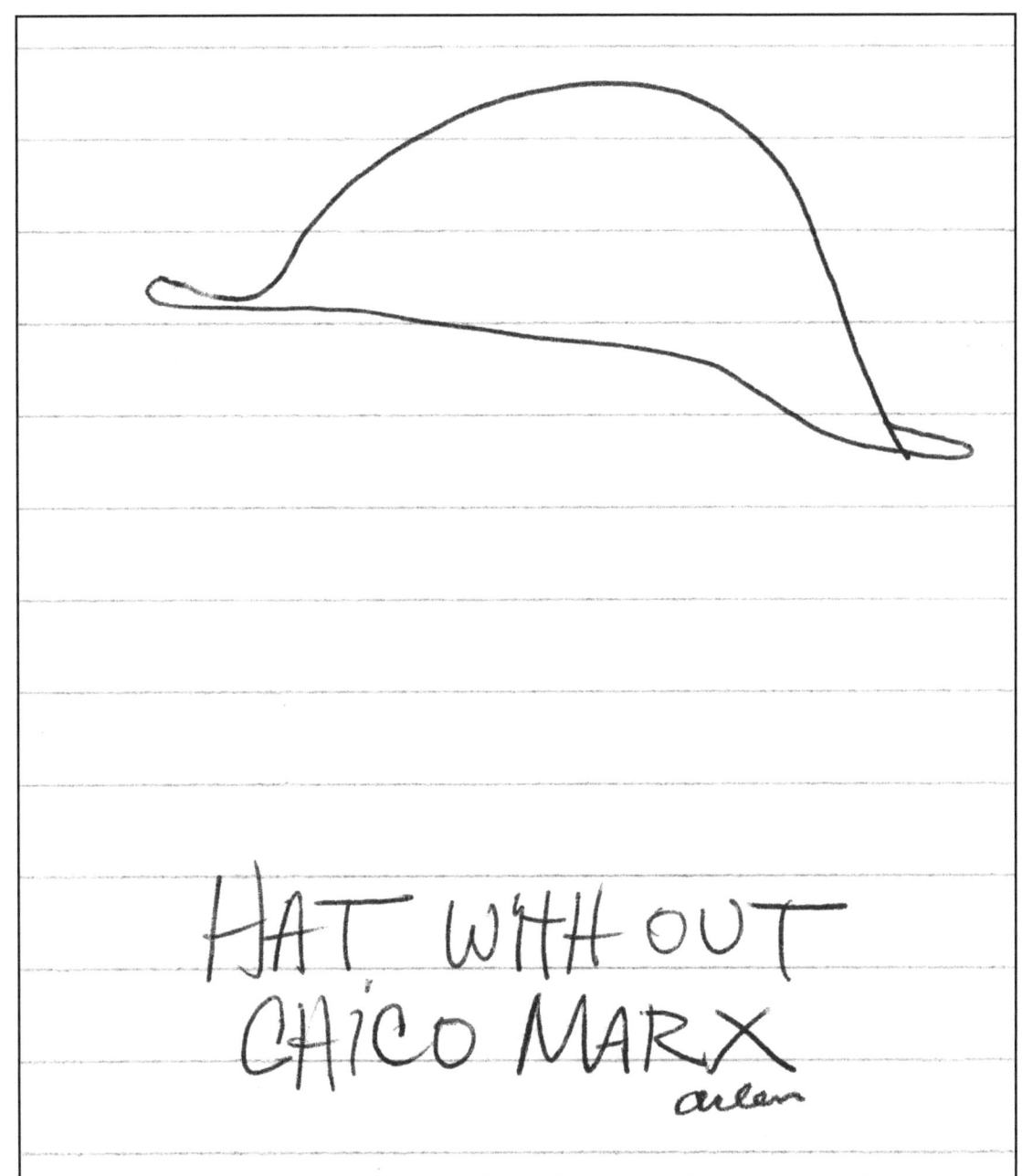

HAT WITH OUT
CHICO MARX
arlen

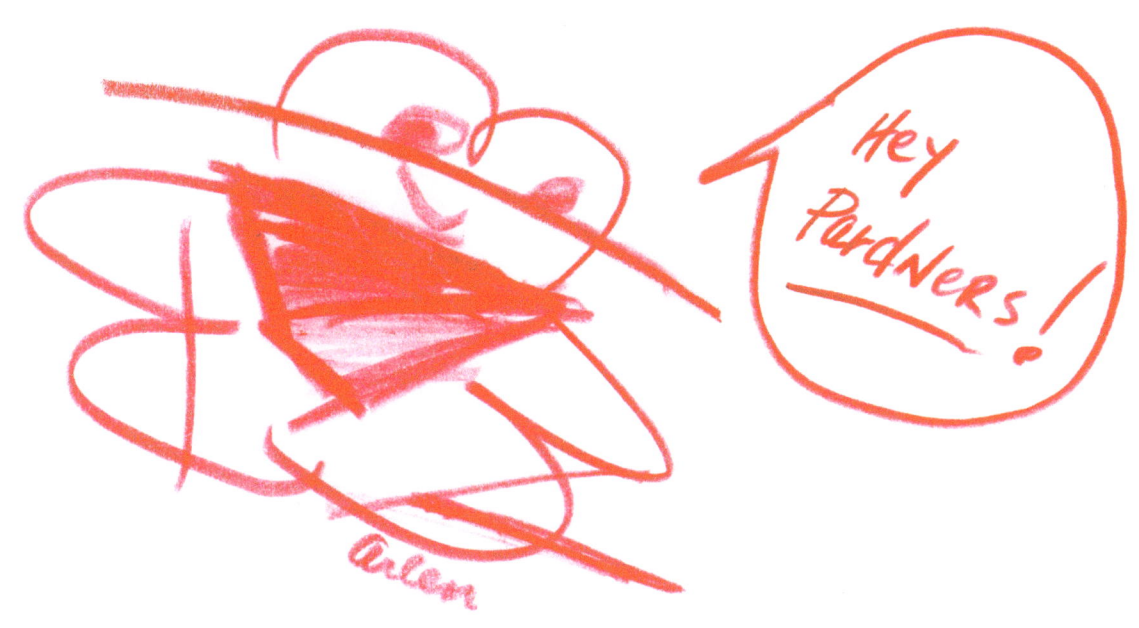

Cowboy Puff
Cereal

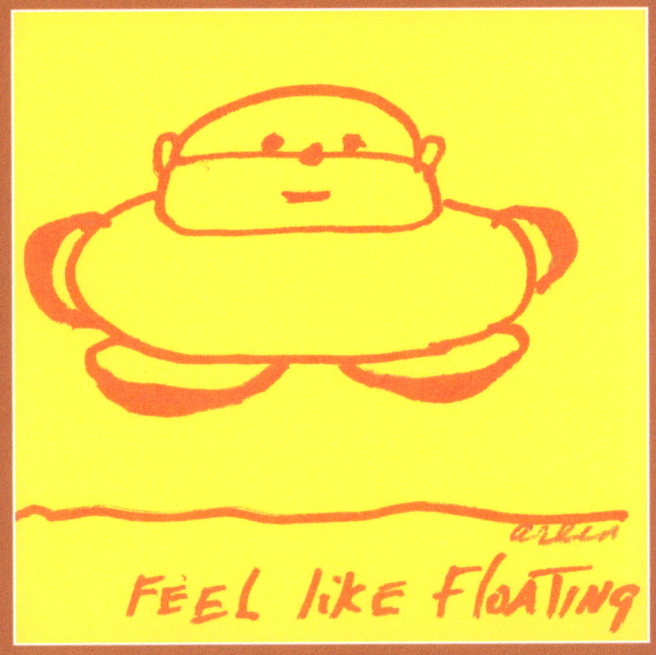

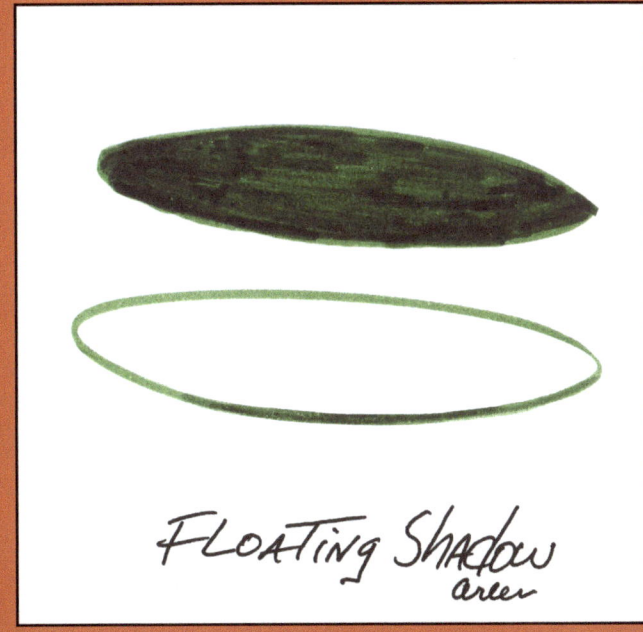

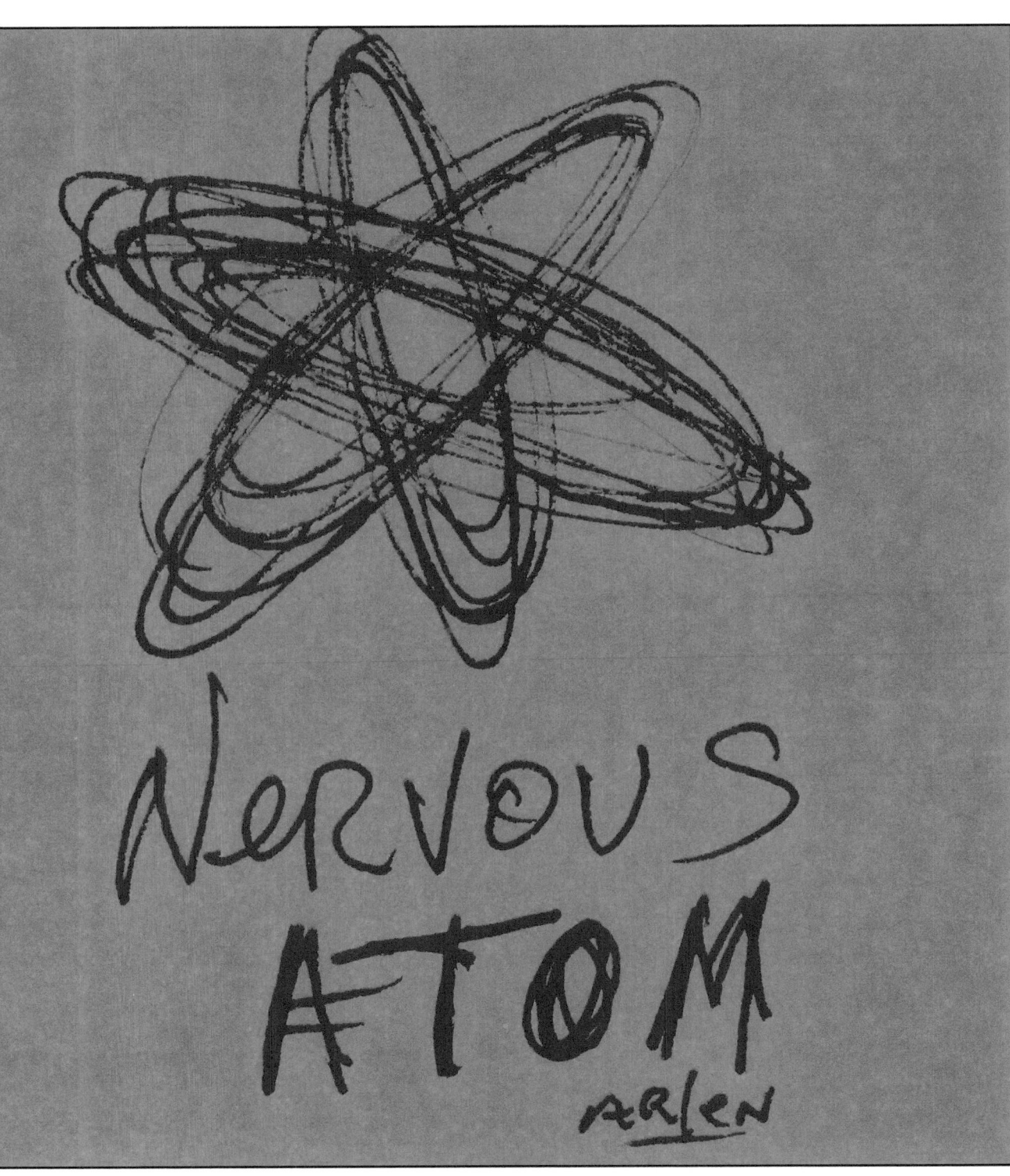

NERVOUS
ATOM
arlen

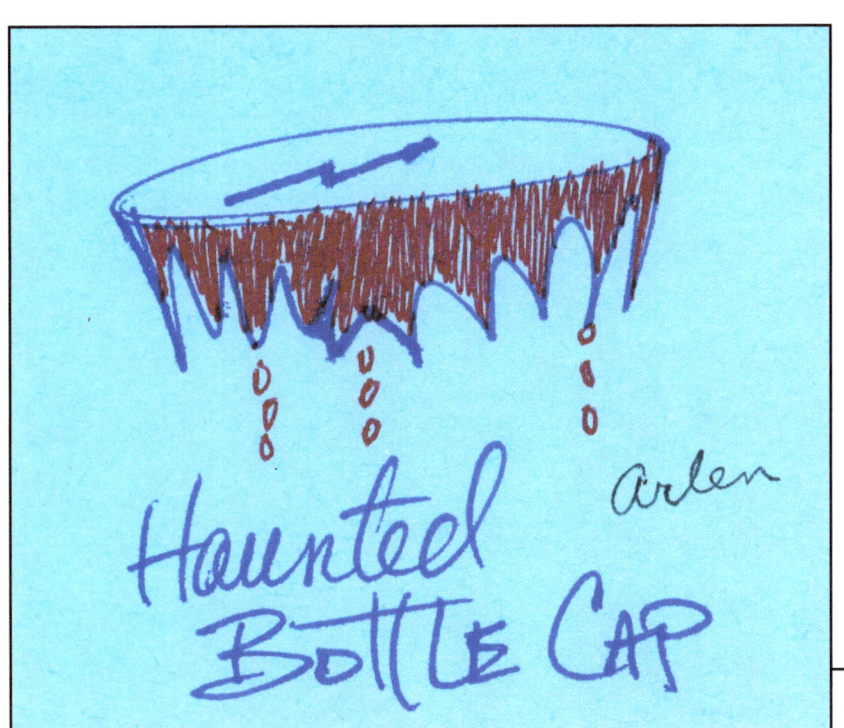

arlen

Haunted
BOTTLE CAP

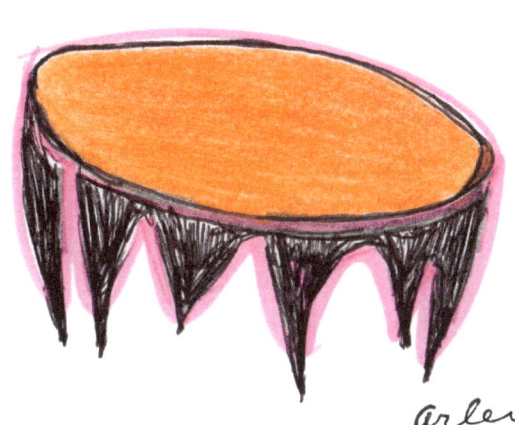

arlen

Haunted
Bottle Cap

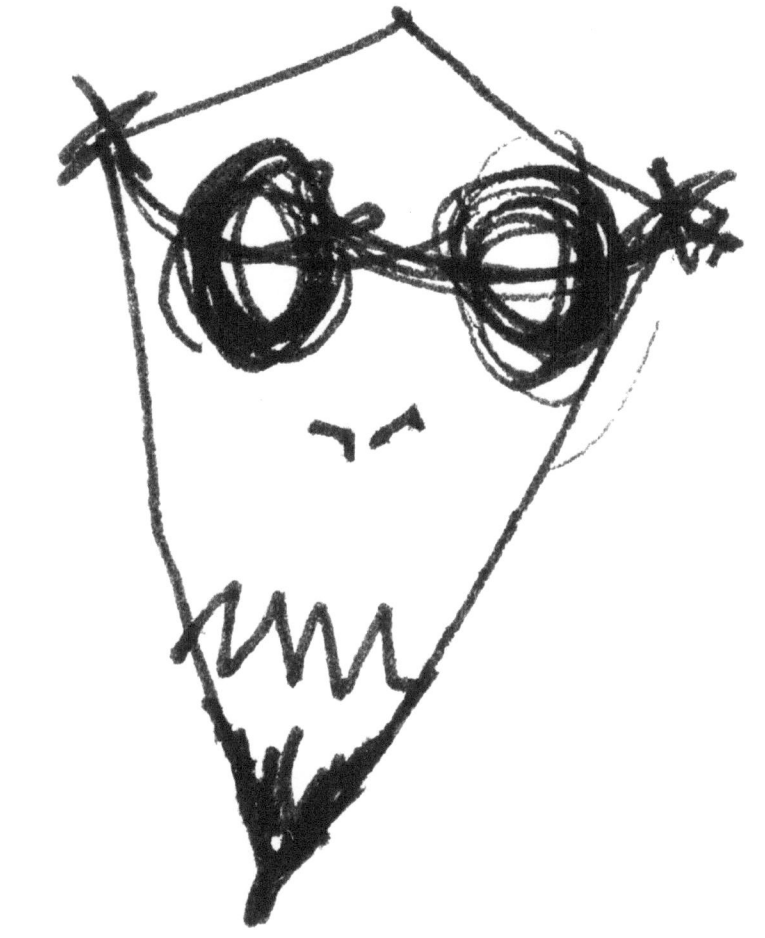

Hip Spook

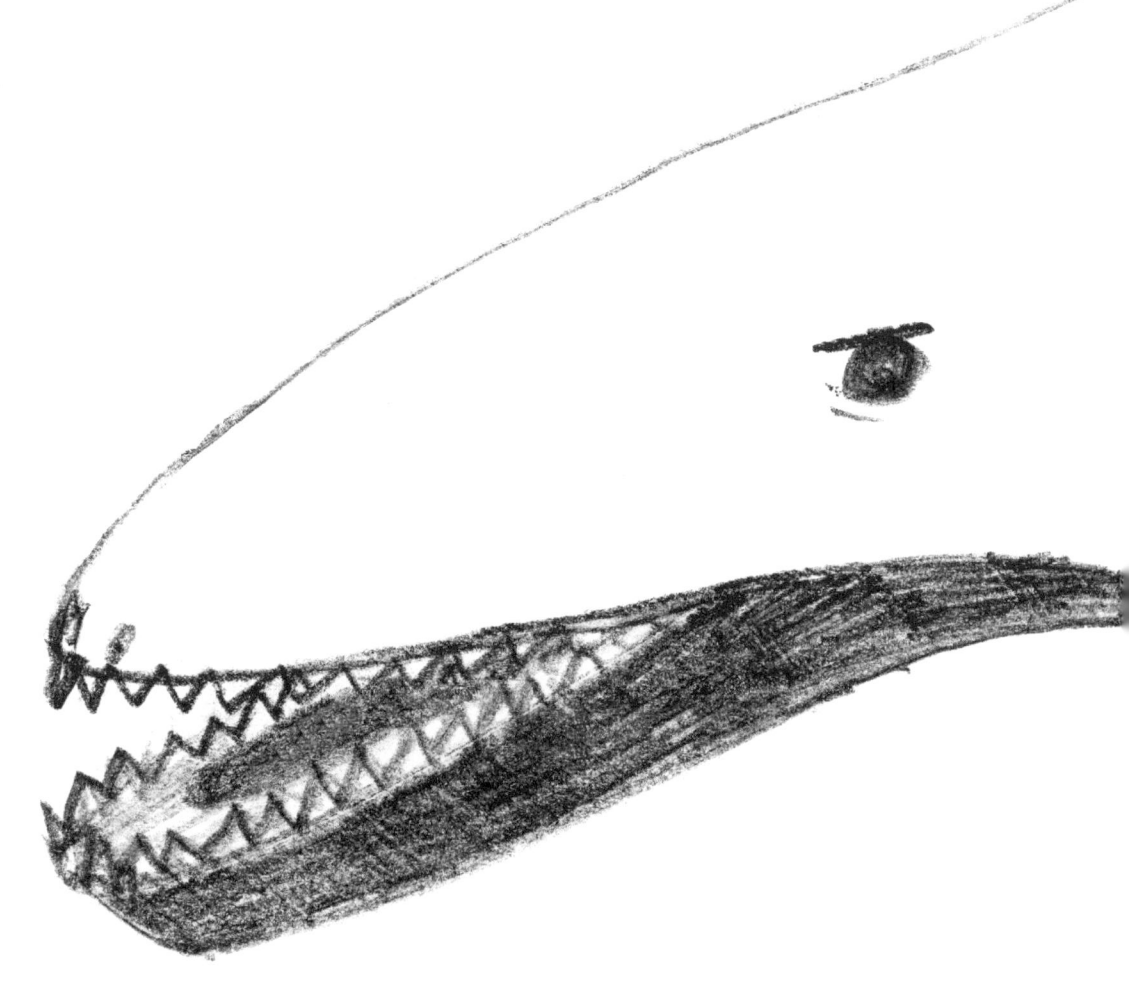

Hello!

arlen '09

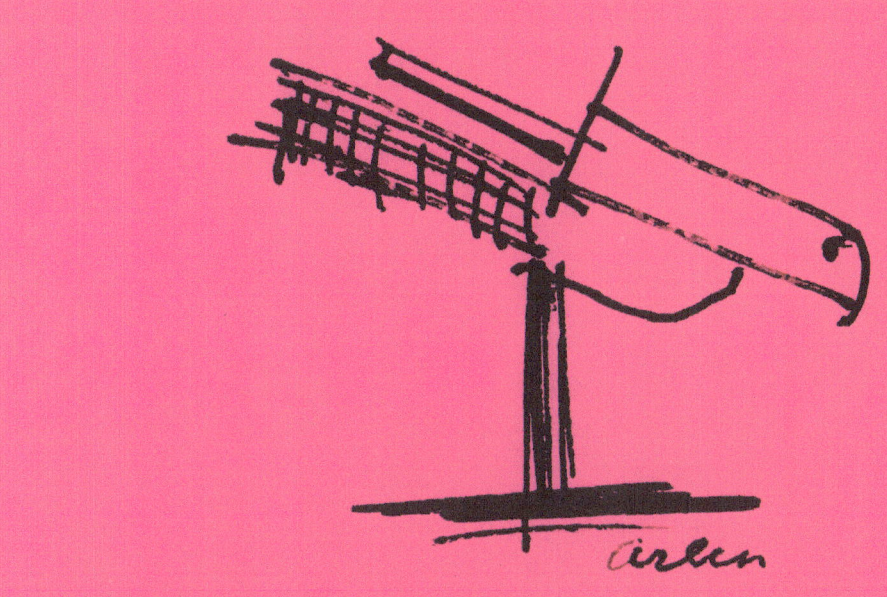

Eagle Mic in
Studio B

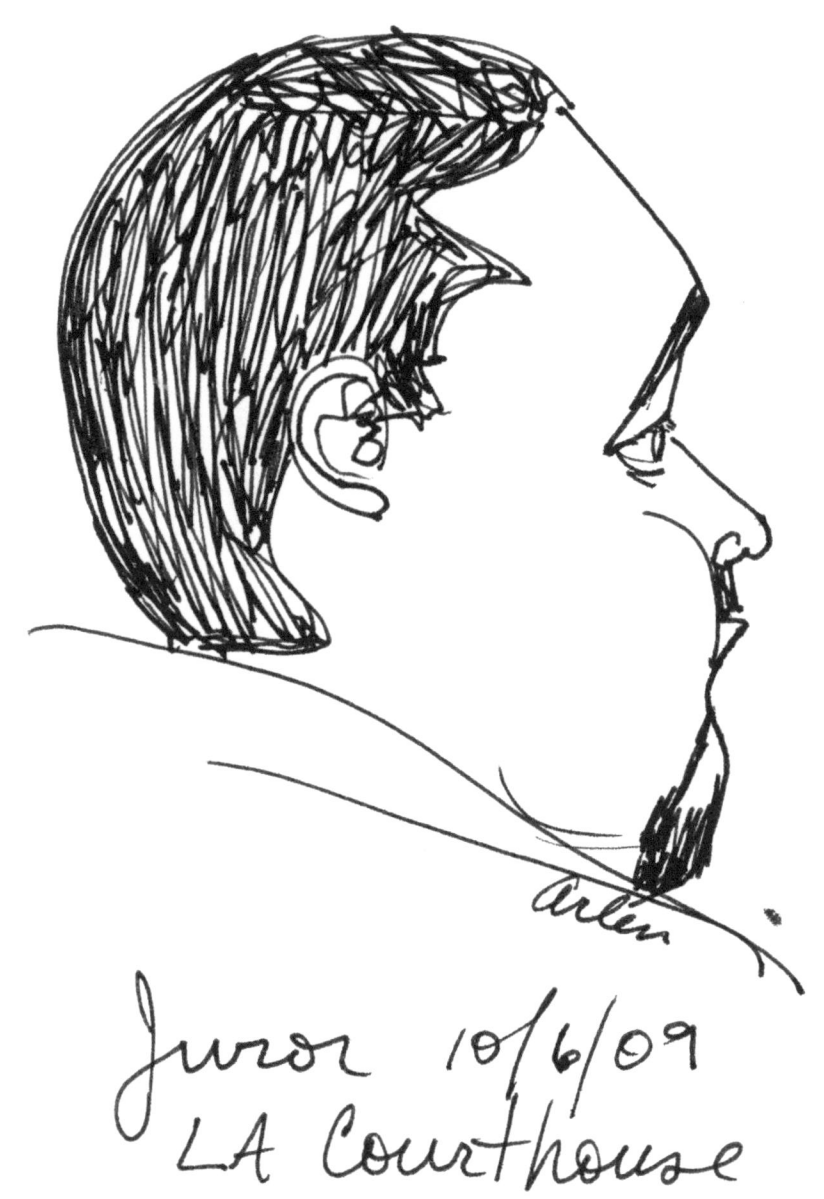

Juror 10/6/09
LA Courthouse

THANK YOU for
purchasing this book!

Please visit
www.bamusers.com
where you can continue
to be *Bamused*.

For book signings please
contact ArlenArts at
email@arlenarts.com.

Good luck and be *Bamused,*
be *very Bamused!*

www.ingramcontent.com/pod-product-compliance
Lightning Source LLC
Chambersburg PA
CBHW050720180526

45159CB00003B/1084